MW01043377

Catching Digital

How to see your future in the digital blur, create smarter strategies for your business, and plan your Digital RoadMap for success

Richard Keeves

Come to the edge, He said.

They said, We are afraid.

Come to the edge, He said.

They came. He pushed them... and they flew.

Guillaume Apollinaire

You have brains in your head.

You have feet in your shoes.

You can steer yourself any direction you choose.

Dr. Seuss
Oh, The Places You'll Go!

What others are saying about Catching Digital

"If you didn't have a strategy for moving your business online before, you now have no excuse. Well explained, informative, comprehensive and sets you up for success on your digital pathway. A great read."

Wayne Spencer
Retail Traders' Association

"The ideas and thoughts Richard Keeves has packed into this book can help business owners build effective digital plans without getting overwhelmed. An essential tool for business."

Jim Wyatt
GM, Digital Economy Branch, Government of Western Australia

"It's not often you see big picture thinking and business planning clearly linked in insightful and practical ways, with opportunity as the focus."

Denny Sterley
Former Australian Practice Leader, Resilient Futures

"This book highlights trends that cannot be ignored. We need to plan our actions and need to create our own roadmaps to deal with business opportunities and threats that are now mission critical. Like it or not they are not going away, and are only getting bigger and faster."

John Clegg
Business Adviser, Omnivest Business Consultants

"There is no question Richard Keeves has a deep understanding of the nature of the digital tsunami that is shaping the way we all live, work and play. This book makes compelling reading."

David Shelton
Director, Transition Capital

"This is a 'must read' before making decisions about technology. Richard explains each digital trend with clarity, preparing you to focus on the big picture of where you are going before deciding on the tools to get there."

Mark Douglas
Managing Director, Francis A Jones

"This book makes me appreciate how much is changing and how much more I need to know. It can be scary, but by better understanding the trends, I can have better thoughts and can better assist my business. This is essential reading. Read it. Then read it again."

Colin Atkinson
Managing Director, CA Management Services

"Compulsory reading for any executive who is serious about understanding how digital communication is changing the world."

James Bull
Business Communication Professional, James Bull Consulting

"As the boundary between the online virtual worlds & our tangible 3D world relies increasingly on our own perceptions, any text we find that helps us clarify the distinctions & how to operate them better is a useful read. Richard Keeves writes clearly, cleanly, & without technobabble. Good stuff."

Annimac
Futurist & Trend Forecaster, www.annimac.com.au

Catching Digital
ISBN 978-0-9808226-2-5
Keeves, Richard

Publisher: Business InfoMedia Online

First published 2010 as Digital TrendCatcher Guide (eBook).
Revised and Rewritten 2012

Published by Business InfoMedia Online, Ground Floor,
11 Ventnor Avenue, West Perth, Western Australia 6005
Postal Address: Box 670 Nedlands 6909 Australia
Phone: Australia: + 61 8 9467 1884

Book and Cover design by Joel Pulido, Business InfoMedia Online

For more resources from Richard Keeves, please visit www.SmarterWebStrategies.com

National Library of Australia Cataloguing-in-Publication entry (pbk)

Author:	Keeves, Richard.
Title:	Catching digital : how to see your future in the digital blur, create smarter strategies for your business and plan your digital roadmap for success / Richard Keeves.
ISBN:	9780980822625 (pbk.)
Subjects:	Electronic commerce--Australia. Information technology--Economic aspects--Australia. Business enterprises--Australia--Computer network resources. Internet marketing.
Dewey Number:	658.800285

I dedicate this book to every business owner and manager old enough to remember there was life before the Internet.

Life goes on, and as Ray Kroc said, "You're either green and growing or ripe and rotting."

If you're still green and growing, and want to grow and protect your business in the Digital Age, this book is for you.

This book is also for Pete, Kate, Jemma and other bright young Digital Natives who take the Internet for granted. What new horizons can you see when you expand your vision beyond today? Find your strengths and your passions, do what you love and create the future you want…

Contents

"What we see depends mainly on what we look for."

John Lubbock

The Digital Blur

"How dreadful... to be caught up in a game and have no idea of the rules."

Caroline Stevermer

Like it or not, the Digital Age is re-shaping the future of your business.

It's no secret that the world has changed massively since the commercial rollout of the Internet over the last 20 years. These changes have created new industries and new global business leaders, and challenged the very existence of previously dominant players.

Who knows what will happen over the next 20 years? Can you predict the future?

It seems there are opportunities everywhere for businesses to create new fortunes and digital empires. Threats and risks seem everywhere too, especially for existing businesses trapped in the legacies of the past or too slow to change despite the obvious warning signs.

How can you plan for change? How can you plan the best pathways for your business when everything changes so quickly? If only we had a crystal ball to see into the future. If only we could see what's coming tomorrow and in five, ten and twenty years' time…

Jeff Bezos, Founder and CEO of Amazon.com recently said businesses should base their strategies on things that won't change.

In a constantly changing world, finding things that won't change is easier said than done. Perhaps it's better to base your business strategies on change you can predict. In a nutshell, that is the purpose of this book.

Some people think their future is pre-determined with a destiny out of their control. I have a different view. Rather than people being victims in a pre-ordained Universe, I believe individuals have choices and can choose different pathways in life.

It's the same for businesses. The individuals driving a business can choose the destination to aim for, and can choose the pathways to take.

As individuals, where we are today is a result of choices we made in the past, and where we go in the future will be a result of choices we make today and on the journey into the future.

We're not victims without choices. Even in a world of uncertainty, if we can look into the future and see what is likely to be coming tomorrow and in ten years time, we can make better choices today.

If we can understand the long-term trends of the Digital Age, we can see the patterns for the future. Sure, you won't be able to see every detail, but if you can see the Big Picture future of your industry, profession and community, you can use this view to plan a better roadmap with better pathways for your business today.

If we can see the long-term trends, it would be silly to ignore them. Trying to fight against them is too hard. Working with the trends and catching the waves they create is much easier and much smarter.

How you choose to work with the trends is, of course, up to you. Different businesses see different opportunities and take different approaches.

Opportunities, strategies and tactics vary even within the same type of industry as entrepreneurs explore niches in different ways that make sense for them.

Fighting the forces of the trends is tough, but cleverly catching and riding the trends can fast-track your business growth and success.

This book highlights 10 Action Principles and 25 Trend waves that have changed the world over the past 20 years and I believe will continue to change the world over the next 20 years. If you are going to base your business strategies on change you can predict, then start with these Big Picture changes of the Digital Age.

The book also outlines a business planning process you can use to create your own digital roadmap. Your roadmap is your pathway to the future you want. It starts with making sense of the rapidly changing and often confusing digital blur.

What's the difference between the Internet & the Web?

Without getting too technical, let's clear this up…

The **Internet** (or Net) is the global system of interconnected computer networks through which packets of data are rapidly exchanged between computers and now other devices.

The **World Wide Web** (Web) is a system of interlinked hypertext documents, media files and other files and applications on web sites accessed via the Internet.

In other words, the Internet is the technical infrastructure and the Web is a system of linked information that the Internet allows us to access. Email, VoIP (Voice Over Internet Protocol) and FTP (File Transfer Protocol) are examples of other systems that can use the Internet independently to the Web.

There is more to the digital world than the Internet and the Web. Digital tools and devices don't need to be connected in order to be valuable, but when they are connected their value and power increases exponentially.

The Internet drives the growth of the Digital Age, and the Digital Age drives the Internet. As digital tools, systems and infrastructure become more useful, faster, easier and cheaper, they attract more users. Businesses move to provide more services and better value online, attracting more people to do more online. New tools are developed. It's a virtuous spiral, and the Digital Age continues to grow, so fast it becomes the digital blur...

earch Engines $$ QR Codes $$
roximity $$ Malware $$ Vir
rketing $$ Robots $$ Video C
mand $$ Twitter $$ Google
ype $$ Phishing $$ Sniffers
rtphones $$ VoIP $$ Peer Rev
PayPal $$ Tablets $$ Automa
Affiliate Marketing $$ Social Me
$ YouTube $$ Open Source $$
WebTV $$ Mobile Marketing $$
pping Carts $$ SEO $$ Faceb
Flash $$ Behavioral Targeting
$$ Androids $$ Cloud Comp
Freemium $$ Semantic Web
cklinks $$ YouTube $$ Privac

Search Engines $$ QR Codes

Proximity $$ Malware $$ Vi

arketing $$ Robots $$ Video

emand $$ Twitter $$ Google

kype $$ Phishing $$ Sniffers

rtphones $$ VoIP $$ Peer Ro

PayPal $$ Tablets $$ Autom

Affiliate Marketing $$ Social M

$$ YouTube $$ Open Source

WebTV $$ Mobile Marketing

oppingCarts $$ SEO $$ Faceb

Flash $$ Behavioral Targeting

les $$ Androids $$ Cloud Comp

Freemium $$ Semantic Web

acklinks $$ YouTube $$ Priva

What's Going On In The Blur?

Over the past 20 years, the growth of the Internet has created new technologies, software programs, services and global business leaders.

New products have entered our homes and businesses, new practices have entered our workplaces, and new phrases have entered our languages.

Every day some new online tool hits the market with new buzzwords to learn and new concepts we quickly try to grasp so we don't get left behind.

It's not surprising all this change is creating a blur for many people who feel they struggle to keep up.

So, let's step back and look into the Blur…

Let's start with abundance.

Abundance, Not Scarcity

With the online digital world, there is no scarcity other than a scarcity of our own time. There is abundance of almost everything else.

Online digital resources are very different to offline physical resources.

In the old scarcity world, the more you use a resource, the less you have of it. It becomes scarce. The less a scarce physical resource is available, the more valuable it generally becomes.

In the abundant online world, resources that are used do not diminish. The more a digital resource is used, the more valuable it generally becomes.

Rather than getting lost in the abundance, a resource that is highly valuable and greatly used stands out in the crowd, not diminishing but growing, and often growing exponentially.

In the scarcity-based off-line business world, large individual firms can generate strength, profits and wealth from achieving economies of scale.

Paradoxically, the same scale that helped these businesses create their wealth often becomes an anchor when they need to quickly change. Their people, systems and work practices can inflexibly weigh them down, and restrict or prevent their flexibility and agility.

It's different online. In the world of abundance online, smart and small highly networked businesses can generate strength, profits and wealth - and stay agile.

This agility comes not from their own economies of scale but from achieving 'economies of structure' using their networks.

These network connections provide the necessary scale with the flexibility and agility to change rapidly for the future.

The online world has tremendous abundance in its resources, information, processing power, application software and storage capabilities.

The most significant abundance comes from the number of people on the network - people who can help you or hinder you and who are often just one click away from liking you or leaving you.

Business that can understand abundance and the power of the networked structures can catch the trends, think ahead and get ahead.

In the online world there is little to stop you using smart technology and systems to enhance your products and services, provide better service for your existing customers, and reach out to new customers in new markets.

There is also little to stop your competitors doing this either, and you may not even know if or when new competitors are threatening your business.

In the global marketplace, new competitors are emerging, cleverly hunting for new opportunities. Even for local businesses, your current customers are not sacred cash cows you can take for granted. Sooner or later, they are likely to be attractive and tempting targets for someone somewhere to attack.

How many of your customers would be tempted by better products and services providing substantially more benefits and value, and delivered in smarter faster ways at lower cost?

Small enhancements can make a big difference, but revolutionary new digital products, services and processes could become game-changers in almost any industry.

There is an amazing array of available technology choices and possible online business solutions.

Paradoxically, the large number of technology options you can choose from is part of the problem. Too much choice often adds to the confusion and when people are confused they typically either do nothing or the wrong thing.

Finding a clear pathway through the Blur is not just difficult, but continually and increasingly problematic.

Many people dabble with new technology and play with fads that catch their attention. They often unwittingly add to the fragmentation of processes and technology within their organizations and the Blur gets worse. Integration of different systems is increasingly important, but often overlooked.

Choosing technology is a puzzle. Many businesses get their new technology choices wrong – or at least, they don't get these choices right enough.

We have to make choices, but staying flexible is critical as what was right yesterday may be wrong tomorrow.

Over time, this puzzle becomes increasingly complex, especially if you get bad or wrong advice from biased and self-serving product vendors.

Your Blurry Picture Puzzle

How hard is it to complete a jig-saw picture puzzle when you only have some of the puzzle pieces and you've never clearly seen the picture you are trying to create?

To make it worse, the edges of the puzzle pieces are unclear and continually morphing, changing their shapes, colors and points of interaction and integration.

For many businesses, the puzzle is just a confusing blur they prefer to ignore; for others the blur gets worse the more they look at it.

How are you ever going to complete the puzzle? Where do you start? What are your options? How do you know what is best? How do you plan the future of your business?

Think about the changes in your industry over the past 5, 10 and 20 years from the digital age. What has changed already for your customers, your business and your industry?

There have been many individual products and businesses none of us could predicted 20 years ago.

However, if we look at the trends and patterns over the past 20 years, we can see long-term change for what it is: generally neither random, ad-hoc, accidental nor faddish.

If we use those trends and patterns to look ahead into the future, it is most likely these long-term changes will continue for another 20 years, if not longer.

You can use the trends and patterns, apply them to your business and your industry and start to predict the future.

Your industry will change and so too will the wants and expectations of your customers. If you can see where the future is heading, you can start to plan your business so you create the future you want.

How could you be doing business tomorrow? What is your Big Picture future?

As you look ahead, your Big Picture view will never get every detail absolutely right. You can create, guide and influence (but usually not control) the plans for the future of your business, but your competitors are a bit less predictable.

A number of your current competitors may already be struggling and dying, some may be asleep, and others are probably evolving.

Some competitors will be a lot smarter than others, and a few could be planning to challenge you, attract your best customers and put you out of business.

New technologies, products and services will emerge to change, threaten and disrupt your business, your business practices and processes, and your industry.

Later in this book, we'll explore how to predict the behavior of competitors. For now, let's explore what's driving the power and growth of the Digital Age.

Ten Action Principles

I cannot teach anybody anything,
I can only make them think

Socrates

Over the past 20 years, I've noticed ten concepts that seem to underlie the growth of the digital world.

These concepts underpin the adoption of digital technology and the Internet, as well as the growth of successful Digital Age businesses. They are so fundamental that I call them the "Action Principles of the Digital Age".

The Action Principles do not just apply to technology. They are basic components for doing business in the Digital Age.

The Action Principles strengthen and drive each of the Trends we'll be exploring. For the moment, forget about technology. Embrace the Action Principles, and you embrace the Digital Age.

The Action Principles are:

1. Simplify: Make the complex simple to use. The digital world is complex and complicated, but few people are attracted to dealing with anything overly complicated.

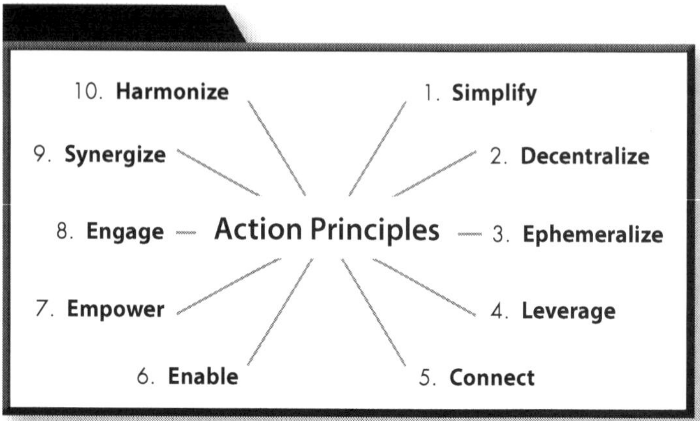

If something offers the promise of value, then the simpler and easier it is to learn and use, the more people will adopt it faster.

2. Decentralize: Resources can be connected together without being located together.

If you can effectively connect many smaller resources in a distributed system you can provide more agility, flexibility and capability to the system.

Decentralizing resources make the system more expandable and more resilient with lower risks than you would have with a large, centralized gathering of resources.

Decentralized systems can usually change faster with less inertia and bureaucratic system controls.

3. Ephemeralize: There is a constant push to do more with less. Businesses have a continual drive to achieve greater efficiencies by progressively accomplishing more and more with less and less, and often at less cost.

(The word 'Ephemeralize' was first developed by R Buckminster Fuller. It may be a new word to you but it describes a vitally important concept.)

4. Leverage: When you can find and use the right levers wisely, your small actions can produce much larger reactions.

You can get better results faster when you find the right levers to give you the reactions you want, preferably with larger and sustainable ongoing reactions.

5. Connect: Connect first before value is expected or delivered. In the networked world, making connections seems essential and obvious, whether the connection is through a cable, a pipeline, or a handshake.

Connections allow the exchange of value, but this exchange will seldom take place without trust being first established. Because of this, your connections must be made and trust must be built well before you try to offer value or take value through your connection.

Connections become stronger and usually more powerful when demonstrable value is exchanged and delivered on both sides of the connection. Over time, connections become weaker if no value flows through the connection, or if the value-flow is perpetually one-way.

6. Enable: Give people the ability to do more of what they want to do; preferably easier, better, faster and cheaper.

As technology forecaster Daniel Burrus says, businesses need to *"give customers the ability to do what they can't do but would have wanted to do, if they only knew they could have done it"*.

Technologies provide tools that enable people to do things. Businesses, products, systems and services enable people to do things. The challenge is to figure out what enough people want to do frequently enough to make it viable.

7. Empower: Help people do as much or as little as they want to do themselves.

Different people are turned on and excited by different things. You need to understand what customers want to do themselves and what they don't want to do themselves.

All customers will probably not be the same, so give them more of what they want, and less of what they don't want. Empower them to do as much or as little as they want to themselves.

You can empower someone by having them learn what needs to be done and learn they can't do it themselves and don't have to do it themselves. Paradoxically, this can be more empowering than teaching someone how to do something if they don't want to do it and will never find the time to do it.

8. Engage: Stimulate more meaningful interactions.

Most of us have too many distractions, competing interests and an abundance of unnecessary information-noise already entering our lives.

You can't expect people to value information that is irrelevant to them or want to endure situations where they are bored, disrespected or not wanted.

Whether you are trying to communicate, inform, transact or simply entertain, there is a need to engage.

Stimulate more meaningful interactions based on relevance, value, importance, timeliness and respect.

9. Synergize: The whole is greater than the sum of the parts.

"Synergize" was the 6th Habit in Stephen R Covey's book, *"The 7 Habits of Highly Effective People"*. It doesn't just apply to people, but also to systems, businesses and networks, especially if you want them to be highly effective.

Covey calls it "creative cooperation", and says it is a process that is part of the adventure of finding new solutions to old problems.

New solutions can rapidly emerge when you join different components, ideas, tools, products and services together. You can create more value with these parts together than the parts each had separately, and use them to create better results together than they may have achieved individually.

All parts are not the same. The power of synergizing comes from joining different parts together, not from having larger quantities of the same parts.

Covey says that valuing differences is what really drives synergy. *"The capability of inventing new approaches is increased exponentially because of differences. Differences should be seen as strengths, not weaknesses."*

10. Harmonize: Individual small waves moving in the same direction can combine to form much larger and more powerful waves.

If you are trying to surf in the ocean, you first need to be in the water. Then you need to choose the wave you want to catch. When you move in the same direction as the wave you want to catch, and get up to speed with the wave, you can catch the wave and ride it.

There are many waves in the digital world. You do have to be ready in the digital water to catch them, but you don't just have to choose to ride one wave at a time.

If you can see several digital waves approaching, you can set yourself to ride multiple waves at one time. Or you can choose to ride waves that are likely to combine themselves in harmony. Harmonizing will form much larger and more powerful waves that can carry you forward further and much faster.

Don't be frightened to join catching big, powerful waves. Look for your own unique market niche and you'll find clear space on the wave with clear water ahead.

As every surfer knows, riding waves is fun and exciting and sometimes more than a little bit scary. The key is to know when and how to get off the wave without crashing into anyone or getting dumped.

If you can find clear space on large waves that are likely to pick up extra energy from the trends of the digital age, you can ride the waves into the future.

Don't just look for large waves. Finding a small wave you can catch and stay on can be just as rewarding. If you can do something you love in a niche you know and use smarter digital strategies to help enough others locally or globally, you can focus your passion and turn it into wonderful business opportunities.

As you move through the next part of this book, remember the 10 Action Principles.

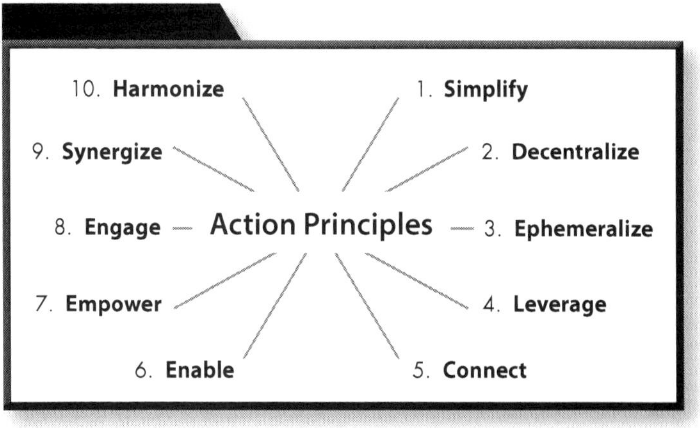

Which Action Principles are most involved with each trend? What ideas do these give you for the future?

It is not the strongest of the species that survive, nor the most intelligent, but the one most responsive to change…

Charles Darwin

Man often becomes what he believes himself to be. If I keep on saying to myself that I cannot do a certain thing, it is possible that I may end by really becoming incapable of doing it. On the contrary, if I have the belief that I can do it, I shall surely acquire the capacity to do it even if I may not have it at the beginning...

Mahatma Gandhi

Plan your future because that is where you are going to spend the rest of your life!

Mark Twain

25 Digital Age Trends

Catch a wave and you're
sitting on top of the world

The Beach Boys

Along with the Ten Action Principles, I've also noticed 25 long-term trends of the Digital Age. You will have noticed some of them too.

As you go through the trends, some may appear so obvious you take them for granted already. Others may surprise you. Each trend is part of the puzzle.

Some trends will appear to be more relevant than others to you as you think about your business, your industry, your competitors and more importantly your customers. Understanding each of the trends can give you insights into your own Big Picture future.

Don't ignore or under-estimate any of the trends. Ignoring the trends doesn't help. These trends are happening anyway, with or without you!

How you see each trend now will undoubtedly be influenced by your past and current thinking and experiences. The opportunities and implications of each trend will appear different to you than they will appear to some of your competitors.

If you want to see the opportunities in the future, you will want open-minded, fresh innovative possibility-based thinking about each trend, not restricted closed thinking from the past.

You don't have to come up with revolutionary new ideas to make it worthwhile. Fresh thinking about each trend can generate small incremental improvements to your current business, systems and processes.

It's Always About Your Customers

Fresh thinking can help you see ideas and options that make sense for you and your industry.

You will see some changes that can help your organization become more efficient in its processes, production and operations.

Ultimately though, real improvements in business are almost always customer-focused and about providing greater benefits and value to customers.

Think about what your customers really value from you, not just the products and services you provide but the benefits these bring to the customer, and the benefits behind the benefits.

Think of the constraints and limitations with your current business model, revenue streams, products and services. Imagine how each trend could change or remove these constraints and limits in the future allowing you to improve your services to your customers.

Successful businesses need to be ahead of the expectations of their customers, but not too far head. You don't want to be behind customer expectations. You don't want to be unable to deliver what your customers want and expect when they deal with you, especially if they can now easily get it from your competitors.

How can your business become better for your customers? How can you make things better, faster, cheaper and more convenient while using fewer scarce resources in the process?

Trends Combined Gain Energy & Momentum

Think of the effect of different trends in variable combinations. Don't just think of a single trend in isolation.

> ***Opportunities multiply as they are seized***
>
> Sun Tzu

Remember the Action Principles. The effect of different trends is far greater when they synergize and combine in harmony with each other.

When your business idea, product or process is in harmony with multiple trends, it gains energy and momentum from the trends. That means you make progress faster and easier, and get better results sooner.

The 25 Big Picture Digital Trends

1: Moore's Law Continues
2: The Internet Is Always On
3: More 24.7 On-Demand
4: Increasingly Faster Speeds of Transactions
5: Increasingly Faster Wireless Networks
6: More and Smarter Mobile Devices
7: Increasing Convergence
8: More Technical Connectivity
9: More Personal Connectivity
10: Increasing Formation of Niche Communities
11: More Linked Corporate Ecosystems
12: Increasing Disintermediation
13: Increasing Transformation
14: Increasing Mass Customization
15: Increasing Globalization
16: More "100% Fit" Products in Global Niches
17: Increasing 1 to 1 Marketing
18: Increasing Aggregation of Information
19: Changing Importance of Physical Location
20: More Low Cost Software & Cloud Computing
21: Increasing Exposure to Popular Mass Culture
22: Increasing Importance of Trusted Brands
23: Increasing Importance of Peer Reviews and Recommendations
24: Increasing Loss of Control of our Personal Information & Identity
25: Increasing Power to Consumers

Trend 1: Moore's Law Continues

- Always more computer processing power.
- Processing power doubles every 18 to 24 months.
- Always faster, smaller, cheaper.

In 1965, Intel co-founder Gordon E. Moore noted that the number of components in integrated circuits had doubled every year from 1958 to 1965.

He accurately predicted this trend would continue "for at least ten years". This became known as Moore's Law.

In 1975, Moore revised the Law to predict the doubling of computer processing power every two years – and this prediction has come true ever since, often doubling within 18 months.

According to Wikipedia, the law is now used in the semiconductor industry to guide long-term planning and to set targets for research and development.

It has also unfolded as a self-fulfilling prophecy, where the goal set by the prediction charts the course for capability to be realized.

As of now, Moore's Law shows no sign of slowing down. In 2008, Intel predicted the Law would hold true until at least 2029. Similar self-fulfilling predictive 'laws' have also been developed in other areas of IT growth...

Some Other 'Laws'

Moore's Law covers increasing processing power and density.

Kryder's law predicts hard disk storage capacity doubling every 2 years; Butter's Law of Photonics says the amount of data coming out of an optical fiber is doubling every 9 months, and Nielsen's Law says that the bandwidth available to Internet users increases by 50% annually.

> ***With Moore's Law, processing power doubles every 18 to 24 months***

Not surprisingly, this extra processing power requires more electrical power to make it work.

The power consumption of computer nodes (i.e. computing devices) has been doubling every 18 months.

Fortunately, the makers of semi-conductors are also focused on processors for mobile devices which use far less power. Nano-technology is already becoming a reality.

In June 2012, a multi-national team of scientists and engineers at the University of Southern California announced they have transmitted data using twisted beams of light at up to 2.56 terabits per second. This is over 85,000 times faster than typical high speed broadband cable today. The futurist website, FutureTimeline.net predicts terabit connectivity will be common for homes and businesses in the early 2030s.

We can continue to expect computing devices to be more powerful, faster, smaller, cheaper and with higher speed connectivity for many years to come. The people who make these devices and the networks we run on are planning for it - and making these predictions come true.

Of course we won't all rush out and buy the latest gadgets, gimmicks and techno-tools as soon as they are released.

In amongst the continual flow of new tools and devices, some will catch on with us and our customers. Some will even change our lives.

We'll try some of these new tools, use them and then quickly take them for granted. Later, we'll discard them as they become obsolete and are replaced by the next great thing.

These days, we just know the next great things will continue to be faster, smaller, more powerful and cheaper - and even more useful.

Trends Closely Related to Moore's Law

When you think about Moore's Law, also think of these trends working in harmony with it:

Trend 4: Transaction Speed

Trend 5: Fast Wireless Networks

Trend 6: Smart Mobile Devices

Trend 7: Convergence

Trend 8: Technical Connectivity

Trend 20: Low Cost Software & Cloud Computing

Action Principles

As you think about the Trend of Moore's Law, think about the 10 Action Principles. What new ideas do these principles give you for the future? What can you do better and smarter?

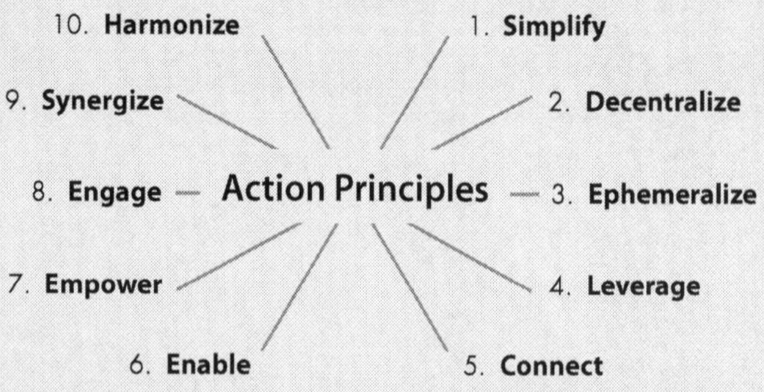

Some Questions To Ponder

1. What do you know about how your customers adopt new tools and systems?

2. How far ahead of your customers is your business in its use of technology? (You need to stay ahead of your customers, but getting too far ahead may be wasteful. Likewise, being too far behind your customers will be deadly.)

3. Have you noticed increased productivity, increased efficiency and reduced costs in your business from your use faster and cheaper technology? How do you measure these benefits today? How could you measure them in the future?

4. How much computer processing power does your business need? Most people don't use all the power they have now. Could you use your processing power more cleverly or could you dumb down your systems in future?

5. How fast and smart are you and your staff?

6. Are you using software tools that seem to make your staff slower or less productive? What is the cause of this? What can you do about it?

7. Which tools make you smarter? Which tools make you more productive?

8. Do your people drive your systems or do your systems drive your people?

Trend 2: Internet Always On

- 24.7 bit flow with more devices anywhere.
- More 24.7 users expect fast response 24.7
- Continual connectivity increasingly taken for granted & relied upon.

If you can remember connecting to the Internet in the mid 90s, you may recall the struggle of programming a modem to dial an ISP's phone number.

Those were the early days of the "Information Superhighway" as it was being termed then. Back then, it was far from a Superhighway.

You usually had to disconnect your phone handset, plug your modem into the phone line and dial up to establish a very temporary connection with your ISP and the Internet.

You would hope to stay connected long enough to send and receive emails.

Perhaps you would visit some chat rooms to find other 'like-minded' people to yourself around the world and share some thoughts and messages.

Out of curiosity, you would 'surf' the emerging World Wide Web, and partially agree with the skeptics who called it the World Wide Wait.

Then you'd disconnect your modem, re-connect the phone handset and use the phone for its intended purpose – to make phone calls to other people.

The point is, back then, the Internet was not always on and we connected to it temporarily.

Even now in 2012 there are people around the world who connect that same way, but for most of us, all that has changed. For the others, it's still changing.

We can be continuously connected to the Internet, often with multiple devices at the same time.

We rely on continual connectivity to the Internet, and already take 24.7 Internet access for granted, even when we're mobile.

> ***In future, anything electronic could have a permanent connection to the Internet...***

We also take for granted that websites we want to visit on the Internet will be available 24.7 and always on.

Some people reportedly suffer physical and emotional withdrawal symptoms if their internet connection goes down or if they can't access their favorite website.

More Connected 'Always On' Devices

Increasingly as new technology rolls out, more and more devices will be Internet enabled and will be always connected.

Sooner or later, anything and everything that is electronic could be – and may be – connected continuously to the Internet.

Data will be flowing between offices, homes, cars, mobiles, alarm systems, fridges, plant and machinery control systems, gaming devices, cameras, signs, televisions, big displays screens, little display screens, projectors… and the Internet.

Look around you in your business and home. Look further to cars, boats, trains, planes, hospitals, sporting grounds…

In future, anything electronic could have a permanent connection to the Internet.

When something that can be connected is made more useful, convenient, accessible or controllable by the connection to the Net, then it will happen.

Where Are Your Customers In The Digital Divide?

The Digital Divide is real, but it's not simply a 'Have' or 'Have Not' dividing line.

When we're connected, it's easy to think that everyone else is connected with us, and it's easy to think that everyone else is just like us, with similar Internet devices, preferences and habits.

Importantly for your business planning, remember that different customers of yours will adopt digital tools and technologies differently.

As every new technology rolls out, different people will ignore it, try it, adopt it, love it or reject it at different stages and for different reasons.

At any point in time with every new technology, your customers will be somewhere in the spectrum of Innovators, Early Adopters, Early Majority, Late Majority and Laggards.

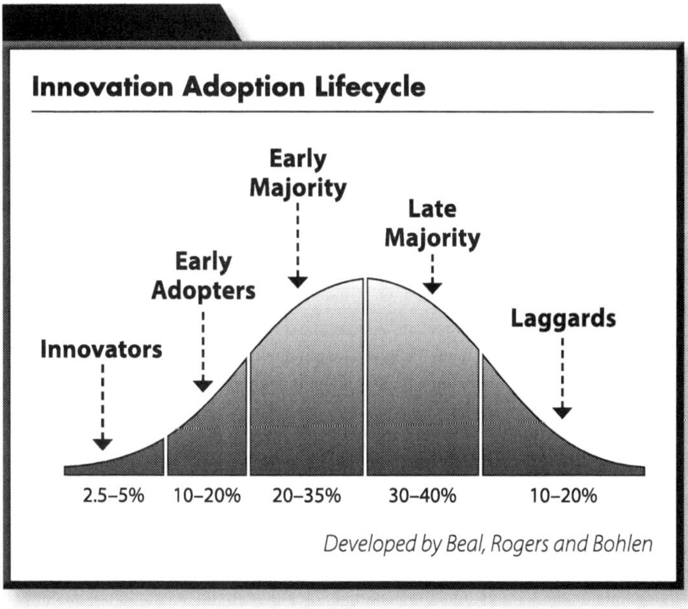

Adoption Stages

1. **Innovators** (May be 2.5% to 5% of population) These are Leaders & Visionaries who will use something new just because they can. "I try it because it is here!"

2. **Early Adopters** (10% to 20% of population)
   These people are Leaders and Trend Followers who typically will try using a new technology or tool when it offers at least one major benefit.

3. **Early Majority** (20% to 35% of population)
   These are Trend Followers, who will use the new technology when it is cost effective, easy to use, provides proven benefits and is accepted in the marketplace.

4. **Late Majority** (30% to 40% of population)
   These people are Demand Followers who will use the new technology, product or service when it is cheap, simple, a mass product and widely accepted by others.

   Often, these people are 'forced' to use something new. In business, 'Late Majority' people may be forced to adopt new approaches and systems by their customers or suppliers.

5. **Laggards** (10% to 20% of population)
   For all sorts of reasons, some people ignore or reject new technology, starting to use it much later than everyone else.

In business planning we need to understand that every new service, product, app and technology you may want to use or provide for others will

1. have its unique set of business benefits that will appeal differently to different customers;

2. have its own unique Adoption Lifecycle; and

3. require its own critical mass of users to make it sustainable.

Maintaining and running different systems for fast-moving and slow-moving customers can become an expensive business overhead.

You want to be ahead of your customers, but not so far ahead that you lose them. Equally, you don't want competitors to come in with a new service that picks off your best customers or the majority of your customers.

The Internet will be always 'on' for more and more of your customers, but they will not adopt everything available to them at the same time.

Many new services struggle to get to the critical mass they need for their survival and growth.

It's a challenge to understand each of your existing customers, what they want and how likely they are to adopt the new services you may offer online.

Ultimately, customer convenience will win, so look for ways to make things less painful and more convenient for your customers. That's what your competitors will be doing.

> ***Ultimately, customer convenience will win.***

Can You Take The Internet For Granted?

Many people are basing key business processes on continual Internet connectivity.

This can be dangerous, especially if your website is attacked and becomes unavailable. Hackers are real and sooner or later, cyber-warfare could affect you.

In the possible event of a large-scale future war, the Internet and many of the networks and servers on it would be likely to be attacked. Parts of the Internet may be taken down, taken out or switched off.

Much of the core Internet infrastructure is in the USA. In June 2010, the US Senate introduced the "Protecting Cyberspace as a National Asset Act".

> ***Many essential business processes now depend on continual Internet connectivity***

This gives emergency powers to the US President to control and even shut down the Internet for up to 120 days or longer with the approval of the US Congress.

Critics have called it "The Internet Kill Switch".

How effective it would be is questionable, as the Internet is designed to route its data flow around any break in the network.

The USA can't switch off the entire Internet but they could take the US off-line by isolating it, stopping internal traffic and blocking satellite communications.

With about 90% of Internet data being routed through the USA and millions of international websites hosted in the USA because it is relatively cheap to do so, millions of business would suffer.

It's a risk, but for the moment, a low one.

What is far more likely is that an individual business such as yours could be attacked. Every day, unsuspecting businesses somewhere are being attacked in Distributed Denial of Service (DDoS) attacks on their websites and Internet-facing servers. Every day some individual or group somewhere is trying to hack into someone else's online systems.

Despite the Trend of the Internet being always on, we really can't take secure and safe continual connectivity for granted, now or maybe ever.

Smart business owners make contingency plans, have good backups of all systems and databases, and test their plans and backups regularly.

> ***Could your business be destroyed in an online attack?***

Trends Closely Related to Internet Always On

When you think about the 'Internet Always On' trend, also think of these trends working in harmony with it:

Trend 3: 24.7 On-Demand
Trend 4: Transaction Speed
Trend 5: Fast Wireless Networks
Trend 6: Smart Mobile Devices
Trend 7: Convergence
Trend 8: Technical Connectivity
Trend 9: Personal Connectivity
Trend 11: Linked Corporate Ecosystems
Trend 19: Physical Location
Trend 20: Low Cost Software & Cloud Computing

Action Principles

As you think about the Internet Always On, think about the 10 Action Principles. What new ideas do these principles give you for the future? What can you do better and smarter?

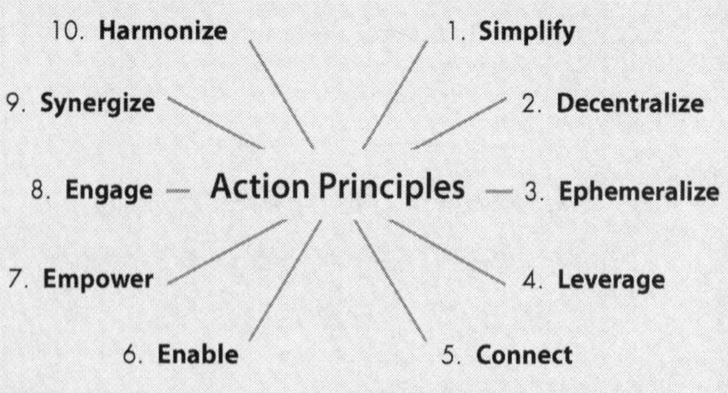

Some Questions To Ponder

1. How much would it cost your business if you were not connected to the Internet 24.7?

2. How would it affect your business if your website was not accessible to others for an hour, a day, and a week or longer? What would you need to do or provide for your customers?

3. What would happen to your business if other websites you rely on were suddenly not accessible to you for a week or more?

4. How would your business operate if you suddenly lost all of your website and customer databases?

5. How reliant are you on email? What happens if your email was not accessible for 1 day, 7 days or 30 days?

6. Do you really want to be connected to your business 24.7?

7. What new services could you roll out that would make life less painful and more convenient for your best customers? What would you need to do get the critical mass of customers adopting your new services?

Trend 3: 24.7 On Demand

- More content is provided and consumed as needed.
- Consumers increasingly expect that suppliers will provide content, products and services when, how, where and as the consumer wants them.
- Requires 'Just In Time' access and delivery.
- Requires 'Real Time' access and delivery.

With continual connectivity comes the increasing expectation that we as Internet users can find and do what we want to online, when and how we want it.

We want to consume content when needed, and we want to be able to research and buy products and services online as we need them - on demand.

The availability (or lack of it) of your product or service online will increasingly influence your competitiveness in the marketplace.

Of course, other factors are important such as your product quality, product suitability, customer service, pricing and the overall customer experience you provide, but for an online business, the time and cost of delivery are increasingly important success factors.

Waiting Time is Measured in 'Seconds'

Off-line, your customers may be prepared to wait hours, days or even weeks to buy and get what they want, but when a customer purchases digital content online, waiting time is measured in seconds or minutes, and not days or weeks.

> ***In the digital world, waiting time is measured in seconds or minutes, not days or weeks***

If a customer is accessing digital content that can be delivered immediately, then the customer will increasingly expect it - instantly, on demand, in real time.

If your customers have a choice of suppliers for the same or similar digital products and you can't deliver instantly, then they are just as likely to find another supplier who can.

For physical products that need to be shipped, the timing and costs of shipping are key reasons for shopping carts being abandoned in the online purchase process.

Having products available to be purchased 24.7 on demand has trained customers to assume fast response times. Product shipping time needs to be measured in days, not weeks or months.

Some leading online sellers of physical products now try for overnight shipping to many destinations. Many include free shipping, not just for the delivery to the customer but also free if the customer wants to return the product.

Organizations who are suppliers of content, products and services need to be geared up to meet this instant 'Just In Time', real time demand.

Smart organizations with effective customer profiles can use the previous buying patterns of customers to anticipate future purchases.

If you can predict when a customer is likely to demand a product, service or piece of content, then you can pro-actively get it to them – or at least offer it to them - before they ask for it.

News sites, music sites, and learning and coaching sites are doing this today, and it usually makes a positive impact.

Even Free Stuff Is Demanded 24.7

Whether customers are paying for something or not, they increasingly have both a desire and expectation they will be able to access it online when they want.

Customers even expect that free products and services they use will be available when they want to use them.

Facebook, Google, Twitter and YouTube are free services but customers expect and demand access to them 24.7.

Paying for something to be available online gives the consumer a greater right to access. Taking money for something gives the supplier a greater responsibility to provide, but really, the money is not the defining business issue.

A consumer who finds a free service to be unavailable will quickly seek out more reliable alternatives.

Just because you offer something for free does not mean you can be less committed to its delivery than you would for a paid service.

There is a widely held expectation by many Internet users that everything on the Net is 'FREE', or should be free.

We tend to expect this, in a similar way to how we may expect shop assistants to freely answer the pre-purchase shopping questions we ask them in their shops.

There is generally very little differential cost in providing online products and automated services at large scale to local or global markets, but personalized service costs money.

The cost of providing high levels of personalized service can seldom be scaled. Having manual processes with tasks for sales, customer-service or support staff becomes a large overhead for online businesses. 'Economies of structure' matter!

"Personalized customer service costs money"

If a customer has a commonly asked question and the answer is standard, then this can often be automated, but whenever a personalized response is needed, there is a cost, and the more personalized the response the higher the cost – in the absence of automated systems.

Some customers are prepared to pay for personalized information, responses and advice but with so much information available through a Google search, many people think they can find what they want quickly and at no cost.

They are often right, as long as they know what they are looking for, but it is easy to waste time searching and not finding.

Filtering the search results to quickly find credible information from sources you can believe is challenging.

Finding quality products you want from sellers you can trust is not easy.

Trusted advisors are emerging in almost every field or market niche. These advisors cut through the information clutter and provide useful and valuable answers, guidance and advice. We will increasingly be prepared to pay for some of this.

The Internet being Always On has led to services on the Internet being Always Demandable.

Before people buy online or offline, they increasingly tend to shop online to do their pre-purchase research. We increasingly judge how good a business is by its ability to provide us with the information we want, need and expect in this research phase.

Customers expect highly responsive personalized customer service that effectively and efficiently answers their queries and quickly solves their problems. They increasingly expect it 24.7.

Trends Closely Related to 24.7 On Demand

When you think about 24.7 On Demand, also think of these trends working in harmony with it:

Trend 2: Internet Always On

Trend 4: Transaction Speed

Trend 5: Fast Wireless Networks

Trend 6: Smart Mobile Devices

Trend 7: Convergence

Trend 8: Technical Connectivity

Trend 11: Linked Corporate Ecosystems

Trend 12: Disintermediation

Trend 13: Transformation

Trend 14: Mass Customization

Trend 17: 1 to 1 Marketing

Trend 19: Physical Location

Trend 22: Trusted Brands

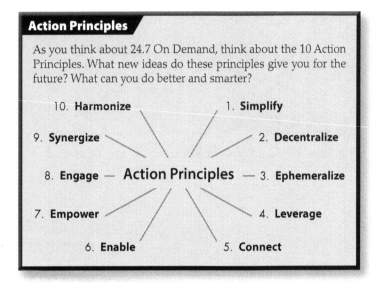

Action Principles

As you think about 24.7 On Demand, think about the 10 Action Principles. What new ideas do these principles give you for the future? What can you do better and smarter?

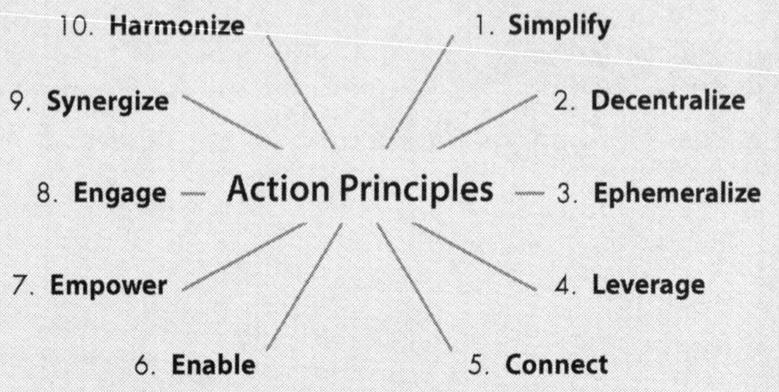

Some Questions To Ponder

1. What additional information, content, products, services or interactive processes do your customers want to access?

2. What would you expect to access or receive if you were your customer?

3. What do your customers want to get from you at times that suit them, but may not suit you?

4. If you can't or don't give your customers access to what they expect or want, who will?

5. What are you doing to become the most trusted advisor for your customers? What could you do?

Trend 4: Faster Transactions

- Actions and reactions at hyper speed.
- Instantaneous transactions become the norm.
- Transactions include Information, Communication, Education, Production and Trading (ICEPT).

The Internet now allows for high speed continual connectivity between devices and people.

It may be tempting to take the new power for these global instantaneous interactions for granted, but look back in time and you see the importance of the trend.

Two hundred years ago a boat coming from England to Australia may have taken six months to deliver an important message, and a further six months for a response to be provided to England.

Just the two-way communication flow of the transaction took 12 months. Imagine if there was more communication needed to take decisions and then take action?

Fast forward to the 20th Century and two-way communication transactions were happening by post, telegraph, phone, fax and then the Internet.

Now, in the early 21st Century, the capacity for instant transactions is the expected norm.

The ICEPT Transaction model developed by Larry Quick outlines the different types of transactions that occur between people and organizations.

Transactions are either Information, Communication, Education, Production or Trading or combinations of these. (ICEPT). All are now done in hyper-speed, almost instantaneously globally due to the use of the Internet.

In the online world, it's not just the transaction itself that is important. The actions and reactions in the transaction processes also need to become virtually instantaneous.

All components in the process need to speed up so the apparently instant transaction is seamless, effective and valuable. Obviously this requires automation.

Just as importantly it requires complete trust in the process and complete trust between the parties to the transaction.

In his ground-breaking book, The R Factor, business performance specialist Leigh Farnell wrote "Trust is the glue of Relationships between people."

In the digital world, trust is not just glue between people. Trust is the quick bonding, quick drying super glue between connected 'things' on the Internet such as software programs, shopping systems, payment gateways, databases and devices.

Intel have forecasted that by 2020 there will be 31 billion devices and 4 billion people connected to the Internet.

In order for online transactions to be fast, secure and automated, these devices need to trust each other immediately and continually.

On websites, customers link to merchants through payment gateways that link to credit card companies such as Visa and MasterCard and through independent payment processors such as PayPal. Faster transactions can occur when these links are automated based on pre-approved trust.

In the world of mobile customers, pre-approved trust between devices allows faster transactions in shops and through mobile applications.

Near Field Communications (NFC) is an emerging wireless technology with transmissions between devices in close proximity – usually within a few centimeters.

This can be used for electronic ticketing and automated payments where NFC is used to connect two (or more) devices.

As an example, a person with a smartphone can wave their phone near a point of sale device in a store and have their funds automatically transferred from the phone's 'wallet' to the 'cash register'.

Other mobile apps are being used to connect customers to banks. An app called 'Kaching' was developed in 2011 by the Australian-based Commonwealth Bank (CBA) for iPhone users.

CBA has recently announced it will be releasing the Kaching Facebook app later in 2012. This will allow customers to do banking transactions while remaining entirely within the Facebook social network.

The Kaching iPhone app also allows 'Bump payments'. This is where money can be exchanged between two people using the app simply by tapping their two phones together.

Trust is the glue for faster transactions between people and devices. Transactions are not just about exchanges of added value. As transactions continue to get faster, how can you ensure you also exchange added trust?

Trends Closely Related to Faster Transactions

When you think about Faster Transactions, also think of these trends working in harmony with it:

Trend 1: Moore's Law

Trend 2: Internet Always On

Trend 3: 24.7 On-Demand

Trend 5: Fast Wireless Networks

Trend 6: Smart Mobile Devices

Trend 8: Technical Connectivity

Trend 9: Personal Connectivity

Trend 10: Niche Communities

Trend 11: Linked Corporate Ecosystems

Trend 12: Disintermediation

Trend 13: Transformation

Trend 17: 1 to 1 Marketing

Trend 18: Information Aggregation

Trend 20: Low Cost Software & Cloud Computing

Trend 22: Trusted Brands

Trend 23: Peer Recommendations

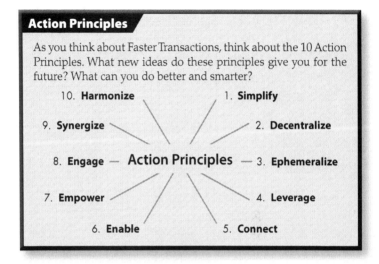

Action Principles

As you think about Faster Transactions, think about the 10 Action Principles. What new ideas do these principles give you for the future? What can you do better and smarter?

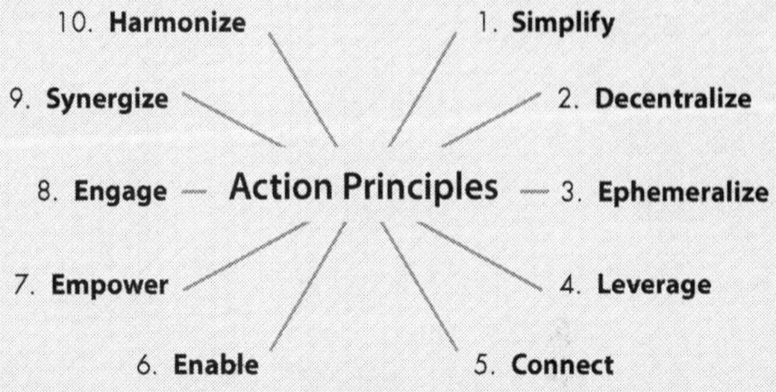

Some Questions To Ponder

1. How ready and well equipped is your business to provide instantaneous transactions?
    - Information transactions?
    - Communication transactions?
    - Education transactions?
    - Production transactions and
    - Trading transactions

2. What instantaneous transactions are already being demanded or expected by your customers? What will be expected in the future?

3. What would you expect if you were a customer of your business?

4. How good are the processes and systems that support your transactions? Are they instant? Can you rely on them? Do they scale?

Trend 5: Faster Wireless Networks

- Enabling Local and Global Mobility.
- High Speed Mobility With High Speed Data.
- Anywhere, Anytime, All the Time.

Gone are the days when we needed to connect to the Internet using a cable plugged into a fixed telephone line.

Now we don't need the cable, or the phone line.

We have wireless routers in our homes and offices allowing many users to connect to share a common ADSL, cable or fiber service. This is provided for free in many coffee shops and bars.

We also have wireless mobile data networks we connect to while we're on the move.

Already we're taking this connected mobility for granted, often only fully appreciating the power of it when we don't have connectivity available.

Wireless networks are flourishing throughout the world as mobile Internet access is opened up for whole regions.

Wireless base stations are capable of servicing local areas handling high speed data, and are far cheaper, faster and easier to install than fixed wired services.

In October 2010, mobile wireless broadband was even opened up in the busy but previously inhospitable trek to Everest Base Camp in Nepal.

Only a few years ago, connecting wirelessly meant being within radio range of a fixed and wired Internet connection.

Now, mobile networks are for mobile users, and allow effective Internet data access speeds in moving vehicles such as trains, cars, buses and even airplanes.

"Streaming video to and from any device anywhere anytime will be taken for granted"

Businesses and consumers can connect productively wherever we are, not tied to any specific location.

We can access content stored in the Internet cloud, send content to other mobile users, and automatically synchronize our smartphones and tablets with our other computers and servers.

The ability to stream video content to and from any devices anywhere anytime will soon become taken for granted.

Streaming will be one-to-one, one-to-many, and many-to-many – such as with joint videoconferences with multiple participants.

There are currently different systems rivaling to be the standards in the 4G tomorrow. 4G is the fourth generation of cellular wireless standards, and is a successor to 3G and 2G standards.

4G systems based around Internet Protocol (IP) allow data to be transmitted in packets as it is on the Net.

In time, 4G will provide much higher speeds with ultra-broadband (giga-bit speed) Internet access, IP telephony, gaming services, and streamed multimedia for users. So what will come after 4G? Generation 5, whatever that may be.

Always more high speed mobile connectivity. Always more empowering and more enabling, and always faster and even more useful. You can predict it. How will you and your customers use it?

Trends Closely Related to Faster Wireless Networks

When you think about Faster Wireless Networks, also think of these trends working in harmony with it:

Trend 1: Moore's Law

Trend 2: Internet Always On

Trend 3: 24.7 On-Demand

Trend 4: Transaction Speed

Trend 6: Smart Mobile Devices

Trend 8: Technical Connectivity

Trend 19: Physical Location

Trend 20: Low Cost Software & Cloud Computing

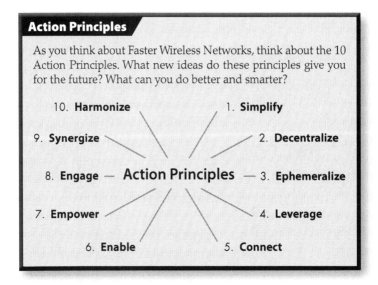

Action Principles

As you think about Faster Wireless Networks, think about the 10 Action Principles. What new ideas do these principles give you for the future? What can you do better and smarter?

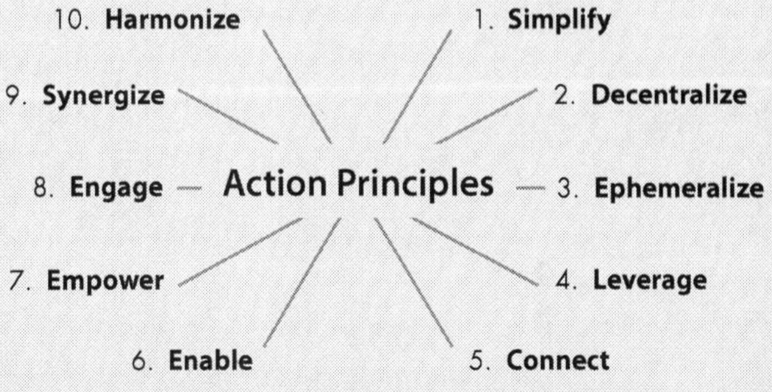

Some Questions To Ponder

1. How could your customers better interact with you when they are mobile? What could they want to do?

2. How do you feel about using video phones? Do you want your clients to see you? Do you want to see them?

3. What capabilities and skill sets do you need to add within your organization for your staff to be more productive when they're mobile?

4. Is there a risk of transferring too much power over your life and business to telecommunication companies? At what cost?

Trend 6: Smarter Mobile Devices

- Smarter, faster, cheaper mobile devices.
- Smaller devices, larger capacity.
- "Whenever, however, whatever, wherever."

Knowing Moore's Law (Trend 1), it's no surprise that the typical smart phone is now a fraction of the size and cost of an old-style personal computer, but with more processing power and data storage capabilities.

The first iPhone was only launched in January 2007, and it's still early days in the world of smart mobile devices.

In 2010-11, the market leader in the US was the Blackberry by RIM, with Apple's iPhone second, and Google's newly released Android phone trying to challenge. Slow moving Nokia missed the boat and was forced to join up with the also slow Microsoft to find a possible niche for its future.

In 2012, the tired Blackberry's future looks bleak, as the fast growing market is dominated by Apple and Android smartphones. Microsoft's Windows Phone 7 could challenge with some promised benefits from tight integration with MS products.

In just a few short years, Smartphone users have come to demand and expect always-on access, very quick boot times; super high levels of reliability and small but clear easy-to-read full color display screens.

An interesting pattern has emerged internationally over the past 15 years. Many mobile phone customers get new

handsets every two years in two year contrá
mobile phone providers.

This means that every two years, these customers have to select the brand and model of their new handset. Some stay with what is good or familiar. Some move to the new 'best thing', and others move to what is pushed to them by the phone company.

The recent sales success of the Apple iPhone has meant that phone companies are not getting the stock levels of iPhones they want. As a result, they are pushing competitor products into the market.

The Tablet market is now booming with Apple's iPads creating a new smart device category in the same way the iPhone did previously.

Google have recently announced their new 7 inch Nexus Android tablets, and Microsoft is coming late to the party with its new Surface tablet.

With this massive growth of simple, small and powerful tablet computers, some pundits predict the death of laptop and desktop computers.

"the smartest businesses want to play leapfrog with themselves"

Many people need larger display screens than the screen of a tablet, and mobile tablet computers in the future could easily connect wirelessly to different screens such as data projectors and flat screen smart TVs.

Look ahead 10 to 20 years... iPads, Nexus and Surface phones and tablets won't exist as they do today. Google, Apple and Microsoft may not exist either... but we can be certain we'll be using smarter and more powerful mobile devices.

It's a changing game, and winners are temporary.

The game is leapfrog, and the smartest businesses are the ones who continually want to play leapfrog with themselves, not just with their competitors.

Making your own products obsolete is far smarter than allowing a competitor to make your products obsolete.

Businesses that become fat, complacent or arrogant because of their past successes seem to be slow at this internal company leapfrog.

We don't know what the future devices will be called or which businesses will make and sell the best of them, but the leaders tomorrow will be smart, visionary, customer-focused and very quick to evolve.

Mobile Apps

There are now plenty of programs and applications to run on their thin, lightweight pocket-sized phone devices.

Apps are being developed enabling an already smart device to do more and become even smarter and more valuable to us.

Designing great apps isn't easy. Making software intuitive and simple for beginners to use can take lots of planning and development time.

If you run a business and want a mobile app, then think about the devices and platforms it will be used on by your customers.

Creating and maintaining different versions of software apps for different phones and tablets is problematic, time-consuming and expensive, and more expensive when the app is enjoyed by customers but given away free.

Smart business owners will make sure their app programmers use programming languages that are'cross-platform'.

A good 'cross-platform' choice today is HTML5 which allows the same business application software to operate on different systems such as the web, smartphones and tablets with only minor changes needed to create the app for each device.

Location & Proximity

Smart phones are getting smarter. Our location is embedded into the device, and our device can be automatically traceable as we move.This can be valuable to us but also potentially more valuable to smart marketers.

Businesses can provide their customers with a friendly app and then send location-based messages to target specific customers differently depending on their purchase history, spending profile and proximity to the business.

It's smart marketing, but the privacy issues will make many customers cautious.

Drive near a bakery and you may get a message about freshly baked bread, still hot from the oven.

Go past the local coffee shop and you might get offered two cappuccinos for the price of one.

Cleverer systems will tailor offerings to fit exactly with your already known preferences – and give you more of what you like. More and more people are going to have faster and smarter mobile devices.

You'll be out of the office, but seldom out of contact – unless you turn off your phone or your battery goes flat!

Trends Closely Related to Smarter Mobile Devices

When you think about Smarter Mobile Devices, also think of these trends working in harmony with it:

Trend 1: Moore's Law

Trend 2: Internet Always On

Trend 3: 24.7 On-Demand

Trend 4: Transaction Speed

Trend 5: Fast Wireless Networks

Trend 7: Convergence

Trend 8: Technical Connectivity

Trend 9: Personal Connectivity

Trend 19: Physical Location

Trend 20: Low Cost Software & Cloud Computing

Trend 24: Identity Control

Action Principles

As you think about Smarter Mobile Devices, think about the 10 Action Principles. What new ideas do these principles give you for the future? What can you do better and smarter?

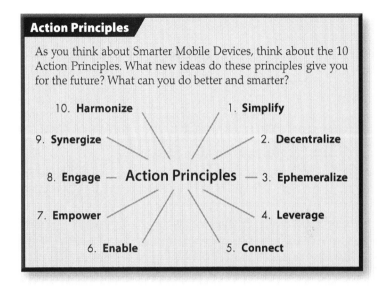

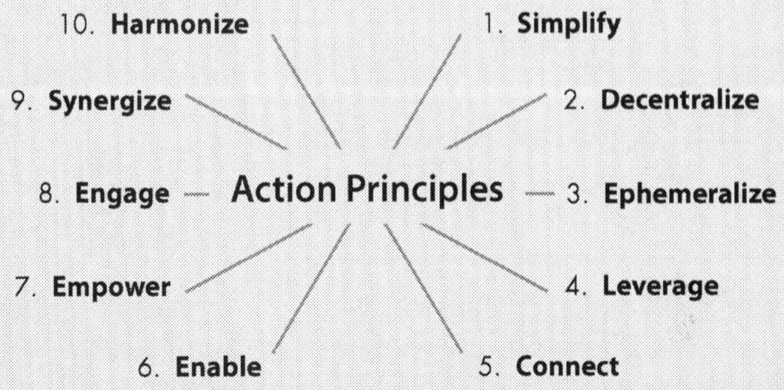

Some Questions To Ponder

1. How can you use smarter mobile devices to better serve your customers?

2. How will your mobile customers want to interact with you?

3. Do you quickly adopt and use new mobile devices as they are launched, or do you wait? Do you struggle to keep up?

4. Are your key customers adopting mobile quickly? Do they wait or do they struggle? How do you know?

Trend 7: Convergence

- The Internet & digital is not just about 'computers'.
- More converging and blurring of devices, systems and content.
- Web, TV, radio, phone, text, audio, video, 3D, Augmented Reality, Holography.
- Mobile interactive multimedia web.

The advances in the Digital Age are re-defining the choices of how we can deliver, access and interact with digital content online.

Increasingly, the devices and the content, together with the access and delivery processes are converging and being integrated.

Convergence is happening all around us, so fast and so much we almost take it for granted already.

You can watch videos and movies on your computer or smartphone or tablet.

You can make free international video & telephone calls using Voice over IP (VoIP) and using tools such as Skype you can talk, watch, text chat and exchange data files while you're on the free call.

You can listen to distant and previously remote radio stations that now reach global online audiences interested in specific music or special interest topics.

You can access news stories online, reading digital newspapers on your smart devices, listening to audio clips and video clips that add more meaning, color and depth to the news stories.

Your mobile phone, iPad, computer, television and even your fridge can now be linked to each other.

Virtually any device can be used to control, access or display data stored on your other devices.

Television programs have time-shifted and place-shifted and are now viewable online, with rich audio and video content no longer being constrained by the broadcast model.

Content is now transmedia and mobile-enabled, and available to be consumed on different devices as and when needed.

Video is the fastest growing segment of the content mix, and online video does not have to be professionally and expensively produced to be effective.

In 2007, two years after its inception, You Tube consumed more bandwidth than the entire internet in 2000, and by 2009 YouTube traffic accounted for more than 10% of worldwide data consumption.

According to SocialTimes.com, in November 2011, Cisco's VP for Marketing and Emerging Technologies, David Hsieh, predicted that web video would soon account for a huge portion of Internet traffic. Hsieh said, *"Today over half of all Internet traffic is video—51 percent. And based on the current trends, we predict that in the next three years over 90 percent of all Internet traffic will be video."*

In 2012, YouTube have over 800 million unique users each month. YouTube's head of global partnerships, Robert Kyncl has predicted that in the next decade 75 percent of all TV channels will be born on the Internet. YouTube are taking it seriously and have recently put $100 million into original content production.

Smart TVs have arrived on the market, allowing you to watch TV, access the Internet, play videos from YouTube and other providers, run Skype video-conferencing and more.

Now you can do all of this on your tablet device, your smartphone device, your laptop and on your TV. And yes, wirelessly in your home or work.

Google TV and Apple TV are being rolled out, and Microsoft TV still may come to the party, albeit late.

Do you think this is changing the game for free-to-air broadcast TV stations?

Spare a passing thought for some of the slow-to-move newspaper publishing companies who grew fat, arrogant and complacent in the past, living off revenue streams from classified ads and other unaccountable print-based advertising. Their game is changing rapidly.

> ***Slow-to-move newspaper publishers grew fat, arrogant and complacent***

Next is Augmented Reality (AR) which is gaining popularity thanks to the smarter mobile devices.

Mobile AR apps use smart features of your smartphone such as the in-built compass, accelerometer, GPS and camera to add geographically-relevant content from the app or the Web to complement the live video being captured by the camera.

Augmented Reality provides a more information-rich experience based on where you are and what your camera is viewing. Is AR part of the future? Definitely. It's already here today.

Convergence has come a long way in the past 20 years' growth of the online connected world. Like the Digital Age itself, convergence has only just begun.

Trends Closely Related to Convergence

When you think about Convergence, also think of these trends working in harmony with it:

Trend 1: Moore's Law

Trend 2: Internet Always On

Trend 3: 24.7 On-Demand

Trend 6: Smart Mobile Devices

Trend 8: Technical Connectivity

Trend 12: Disintermediation

Trend 13: Transformation

Trend 18: Information Aggregation

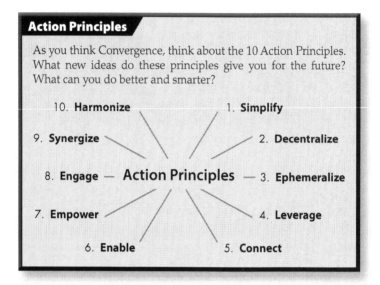

Action Principles

As you think Convergence, think about the 10 Action Principles. What new ideas do these principles give you for the future? What can you do better and smarter?

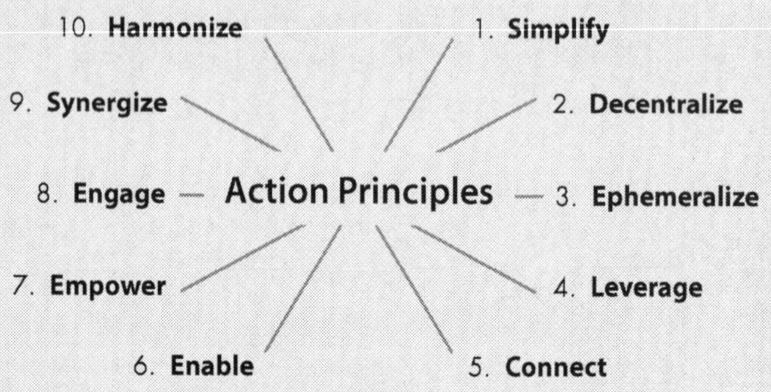

Some Questions To Ponder

1. How can you use ongoing convergence to add value to your customers?

2. How can you use videos as tools in your sales, marketing and customer support?

3. How do your customers use YouTube? How can you be there for them, with messages they want and need?

4. Will your customers expect videos rather than text-based information such as product manuals?

5. Have you considered Augmented Reality?

Trend 8: Technical Connectivity

- The 'Internet of Things'.
- Integration of networks, systems, applications, databases, devices, authorizations & access codes.
- More Things become electronic and almost anything electronic can be connected.
- More reliance on the Cloud.

Think of Technical Connectivity as networked connections between Things rather than people. Think of a Thing as any device that can be given a unique Internet address.

These Things may be real and physical devices like a web-camera, phone, Internet-enabled fridge, laptop computer, or a switch connected to the Internet to control your home or office air-conditioning.

> ***Connectivity of devices leads to remote control of devices and processes***

In addition to real Things, virtual Things that only exist inside a computer such as resources, software or databases can be connected and integrated together.

Remote Control

Connectivity of devices leads to remote control of those devices, and remote control over processes in which those devices are part.

Traffic Monitoring & Smarter Navigation

Video cameras are being set up to view traffic flows. Monitoring is done remotely in controls rooms by operators able to control traffic lights and change messages on electronic warning signs along the roadways.

Individuals can monitor these same cameras over the Web or on their mobile phones. Smart integration with the car navigation systems allows in-car displays to not only show the view of traffic up ahead, but also to suggest better routes for faster trips.

Internet Hunting

In 2005, the first Internet hunting website, Live-Shot.com was set up using remotely controlled firearms. These can be aimed using webcams and triggered remotely by online control systems.

Initially created to 'provide an authentic hunting experience for disabled persons', the concept has now been banned in most states of the USA.

WebRelay

WebRelay from ControlByWeb.com is an electrical relay (or electrical switch) with a built-in web server. The relay can be turned on, off, or pulsed using a web browser.

According to its makers, it already has a long history of reliable operation in many applications including industrial control, pump and motor control, security lock systems, remote reboot, lighting control, weather sensors and remote control and monitoring.

"Add a light switch in your home that controls the lights at the office across town. Put a button in your office that locks or unlocks your other office three blocks away.

Connect a WebRelay unit to a door sensor at your office, factory, store, etc. Connect a chime to another WebRelay unit in your home. Each time the door at the office, is opened, you are alerted with a chime. If the door is opened when nobody should be there, you can immediately check things out using a remote video camera."

These are simple applications. What could you control remotely in your business? What would your customers like to control?

WeatherViz

We can already watch satellite imagery and view webcams of beaches to monitor surf conditions but the three dimensional moving sculpture (or kinetic sculpture) WeatherViz takes presentation of data to another level.

Weatherviz is an environmental data-driven kinetic sculpture which uses a data-stream of Internet downloaded weather information to drive four dynamic components of the sculpture.

Representing precipitation, velocity, weather energy and temperature, each component in the sculpture moves in according to real data from live weather events.

Private Digital Networks

This connectivity does not need to happen using the Internet as private computer and telecommunications networks allow private and often more secure connectivity and control.

Virtual Private Networks (VPNs) can be established over the Internet to provide greater privacy and security of data flow but without the higher costs of a totally private network.

Private networks and VPNs are being used for the remote monitoring and control of complex processes.

Remote Mining

Mining and resource companies are starting to monitor and control equipment remotely. Mining giant Rio Tinto has established a "mine of the future" control centre in Perth, Western Australia to remotely manage the automated operation of its iron ore mines in Australia's Pilbara region, some 1,500km away.

Fixed plant and equipment can be monitored and Rio is launching remotely controlled trucks and even trains.

According to Rio Tinto, the system uses high precision global positioning satellite (GPS) technology, advanced machine control communication systems, laser and radar systems; real time safety monitoring of personnel and equipment using proximity detection; and remote expert human support and planning systems.

The trucks travel along pre-defined routes. The vehicles receive data about the location, speed and direction of all vehicles nearby and can adjust their own speed based on that information.

> ***Mining employees will work like air traffic controllers***

"Employees will work like air traffic controllers. They will supervise the automated production drills, loaders and haul trucks from a remote operations centre in Perth." (Source: Rio Tinto)

Connected Identities

Increasingly, devices and applications will have our identity embedded in them for automated recognition and access. This can obviously present risks if the device is stolen.

Different websites are now sharing Identity Access Management systems to allow users to have one identity across different sites.

Today, Open ID, Facebook, Twitter or Google Gmail identities can be used to gain access to different third party sites without having to create new identities on these sites.

The connected Identity Access Management systems utilize the user's unique user name and password combination to authenticate and then be granted or denied access rights to data and resources on the third party site.

For Facebook and Google, it's a strategy to dominate and own the user's behavioral data as well as their personal information. Most users don't realize the behavior and online activity can be tracked so easily.

From the customer's perspective, the shared or common Identity Access Management systems give a Single Sign On (SSO) which provides a faster, easier and more seamless experience as the customer moves between different sites.

Sharing Identity Access Management systems is already raising privacy issues with greater risks from the real and growing issue of identity theft.

As mentioned earlier, Intel have forecasted that by 2020 there will be 31 billion devices and 4 billion people connected to the Internet.

The Internet of Things is big already, and going to be huge. What will you be able to do with it?

Trends Closely Related to Technical Connectivity

When you think about Technical Connectivity, also think of these trends working in harmony with it:

Trend 1: Moore's Law

Trend 2: Internet Always On

Trend 3: 24.7 On-Demand

Trend 4: Transaction Speed

Trend 5: Fast Wireless Networks

Trend 6: Smart Mobile Devices

Trend 7: Convergence

Trend 9: Personal Connectivity

Trend 11: Linked Corporate Ecosystems

Trend 12: Disintermediation

Trend 17: 1 to 1 Marketing

Trend 18: Information Aggregation

Trend 20: Low Cost Software & Cloud Computing

Trend 24: Identity Control

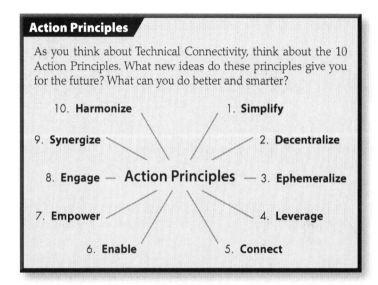

Action Principles

As you think about Technical Connectivity, think about the 10 Action Principles. What new ideas do these principles give you for the future? What can you do better and smarter?

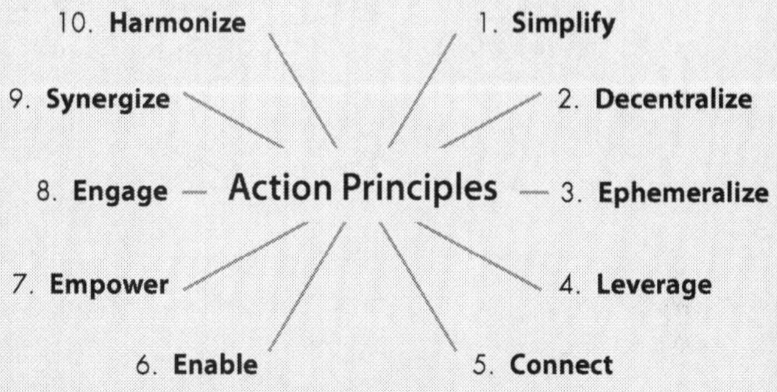

Some Questions To Ponder

1. How could you add value to your customers by allowing them to connect more directly with you? What could you then do better, faster, stronger or cheaper?

2. What Things could you connect to through the Internet or other networks to help your business?

3. What Things do you have that your customers might like to connect to? How would that help them?

4. How you make your business more productive and more profitable through smarter technical networking?

5. What Things could you connect together to create new products or services?

Trend 9: Personal Connectivity

- More social networking.
- Expanded networks include more friends who have never met but who implicitly trust each other's opinions.
- Requires authenticity.
- Quality will trump Quantity for most networks.

This Personal Connectivity trend is about more and more people connecting online – and sharing and collaborating in new and increasingly valuable ways.

This won't be news to you, but it's important to understand and work with the trend. So what's happening?

Using the Internet, individuals and groups located anywhere can connect together, wherever and whenever they want.

These connections and exchanges between people may occur at the same time in an immediate and synchronous communication.

Or messages may be added by one person and then viewed and responded to by another person or group at a later time in an asynchronous communication.

Not only that, but the messages created and added by one person can easily be passed on to others and are almost impossible to remove.

Every message created adds to the digital footprint of the message creator, over time forming a detailed digital profile of the individual creator.

The ability for like-minded people with common interests to connect personally online and collaboratively share has evolved over the past 20 years and will continue to evolve in the future.

From the early discussion groups, forums, bulletin boards and gaming environments, we now connect with today's social networking platforms such as Facebook and LinkedIn; photo and video sharing platforms such as YouTube, Flickr and Instagram; and online virtual worlds such as Second Life.

Today's largest and most well known example is Facebook, which claims 901 million monthly active users at the end of March 2012 (as reported by Facebook in July 2012.)

According to Facebook, it had more than 125 billion friend connections on Facebook at the end of March 2012. With 900 million users, on average every Facebook user has 139 friends.

On average more than 300 million photos were uploaded to Facebook every day in the three months ended March 31, 2012. That's a lot of photos... and a lot of private personal information being shared online.

The numbers are staggering, and with such size, it might be tempting to think that Facebook's future is assured in the Digital Age.

Tempting... but probably wrong. No business has an assured future, especially one that occasionally treats its valuable users with contempt. Even non-paying customer users deserve respect.

Facebook users don't pay money to access the platform, but rather they pay by providing their personal information which Facebook turns into valuable profile-based targeted advertising opportunities.

Most Facebook users don't realize it, but they - or we - are the product of Facebook. Access to us based on our personal information is the product Facebook sells to its paying customers.

Facebook's track record of respectfully handling that personal information has been woeful.

> ***No business has an assured future, especially if it treats its valuable users with contempt***

According to Facebook founder Mark Zuckerberg, with the rise of social networking online people no longer have an expectation of privacy. It's sad if he is right, but I disagree with him and think his view is entirely self-serving.

Facebook has a history of leaking personally identifiable information to third parties. Facebook has also shown itself to be tricky and manipulative in its privacy management practices.

Recently floated on NASDAQ with a valuation of $104B, and annual profit of about $1B, Facebook will now be under enormous pressure to make more money to keep investors happy.

Given Facebook's need for greater profits and lack of care about privacy, this raises greater risks for Facebook users and does little to assure its future as a Digital Age Giant.

A lot of Facebook users don't care about privacy, don't think about privacy or don't understand their Facebook privacy settings.

Information that you or your kids put into Facebook can easily end up anywhere, anytime and forever.

The website WeKnowWhatYoureDoing.com searches Facebook's public content for status update messages containing specific keywords, and automatically presents these messages together with the Facebook user's photo and name.

Categories in this site include 'Who wants to get fired?' which displays messages that include the keyword phrase 'I hate my boss'. Other categories are 'Who's hungover?'; 'Who's taking drugs?' and 'Who's got a new phone number?'

Once released, information online can go anywhere. It's scary when you think about it.

Social Media and Your Return on Investment

Many businesses are currently struggling to use social media effectively and to get a good Return On Investment (ROI) from it.

Social Media Fatigue is a syndrome being felt by many businesses who find running social media marketing involves too much work and time for the results they observe and achieve.

Many also feel fatigue from a constant need to use, refresh and update their various social media systems. Some give up.

Social media marketing is a long term process, based on joining in and stimulating conversations, engaging with customers and followers, building trust, adding value and providing support.

Recruitment Companies & Headhunting

Sectors such as recruitment generate good ROI using Facebook and LinkedIn, but many others don't.

The heavy use of social media by recruitment companies creates other risks to vulnerable businesses whose staff profiles are publicly available, raising opportunities for good employees to be head-hunted and poached.

Social Media Policies

Developing appropriate social media policies and practices is important.

As the business owner you can maintain some control of what your staff say and do in social media, but you will never have total control. Better to have responsible staff who know the ground rules for acceptable behaviors.

A key word in the world of social networking is 'authenticity'. There is no point encouraging social networks in your business and being involved with social media if you won't allow your staff to be open, real and genuine about your business.

Monitoring what is being said about business in social media is becoming more important. Word of mouth comments spread by your customers and your staff may be either positive or negative.

Knowing what is being said about you allows you to constructively and appropriately respond.

> ***Social conversations can't be controlled***

Building Trust

In the online world, consumers need to know they can trust a business.

Trust is seldom based on what the business owner or brand manager says but rather what other customers say about it.

For many consumers, comments from friends and even strangers in social media have become a crucial aspect of the decision making process about what to buy and from whom.

Social conversations can't be controlled. Involvement with integrity takes time. Don't be defensive. Use feedback to improve.

Once something is in social media on the web, assume it is there forever. It may never be forgotten. Encourage your staff to think first and ask this question before they say something about your business in a social media platform "Will it help our business or hurt our business if one thousand prospective customers see this?"

Trends Closely Related to Personal Connectivity

When you think about Personal Connectivity, also think of these trends working in harmony with it:

Trend 2: Internet Always On

Trend 4: Transaction Speed

Trend 6: Smart Mobile Devices

Trend 8: Technical Connectivity

Trend 10: Niche Communities

Trend 11: Linked Corporate Ecosystems

Trend 12: Disintermediation

Trend 17: 1 to 1 Marketing

Trend 21: Popular Mass Culture

Trend 22: Trusted Brands

Trend 23: Peer Recommendations

Trend 24: Identity Control

Trend 25: Consumer Power

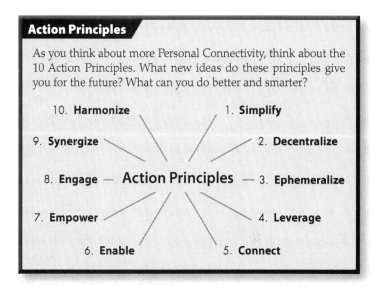

Action Principles

As you think about more Personal Connectivity, think about the 10 Action Principles. What new ideas do these principles give you for the future? What can you do better and smarter?

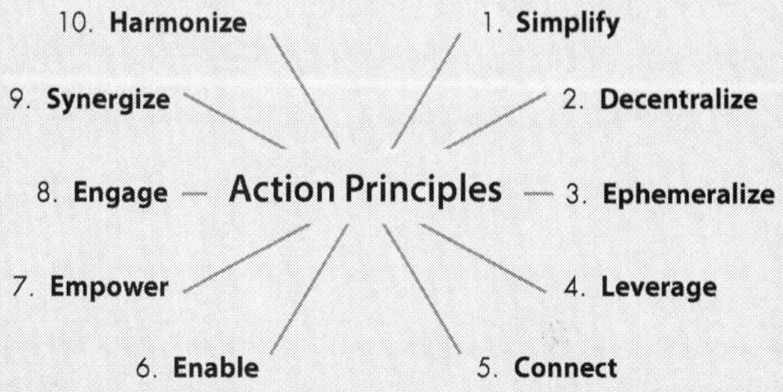

Some Questions To Ponder

1. How successful is your business at using social media?

2. Do you actively encourage more personal connectivity between your staff and your customers?

3. What value can you add to your customers through meaningful conversations using online social networks?

4. What information is public now in social networks about you, your family or your business that could be damaging you and may haunt you forever? How do you know?

Trend 10: Niche Communities

- **"Birds Of A Feather Flock Together."**
- **Communities form, trust develops.**
- **Communities can become markets.**
- **Macro communities and Micro-communities**
- **Connect, Join, Belong, Contribute, Add Value, Be Valued.**

Communities are widespread across the online world, and have been since the very early online days. This trend has been growing for over 40 years.

The Birth of Online Communities

As early as 1969, the computer network that became the Internet was used by groups of academics at different universities in the USA to share their thoughts and views on research projects.

Usage grew amongst academics globally, and when the Internet was opened up for commercial use in the early 1990s, there were already thousands of small groups discussing specific topics of interest.

These groups or communities have continued to form and flourish, and online meeting spaces have evolved with changing technology and platforms.

The early days of UseNet newsgroups have now been replaced by groups that form on peer to peer networks, email lists, special interest websites, large search engines and directories and social media platforms.

The old UseNet newsgroups have been migrated into Google Groups. Facebook, Yahoo and LinkedIn all run different Groups.

At first glance, groups may appear to simply be places for online discussions where people can seek help, raise questions and debate subjects of mutual interest.

These various groups, forums and other meeting places can be vitally important for you as you plan your digital future as these groups can become the homes for online communities.

There are millions of groups online. Within any niche you can imagine, there are probably dozens of groups serving the niche community.

Start by identifying the niche communities relevant to your business. Find the various places these communities congregate online.

Join them, belong to them and contribute to them. When you add value to the people in these groups, you will become valued within the group.

Become The Trusted Advisor

Smart online marketers find, join or create community groups in the field of business.

They contribute to the community with help and advice and over time strive to build trusted relationships within these groups.

As a result, the online community becomes the marketplace for the trusted community advisor who now becomes a trusted supplier.

When new members join the community, existing members will often recommend the trusted advisor as someone to turn to for help.

If the trusted advisor has built a solid reputation within that community based on sincere and valuable help, the positive reviews and ratings make a powerful and demonstrable track record of goodwill. The advice you have provided becomes an ever-present historic record of your value.

"Crass and ineffective marketers crash their way into these online groups and communities."

Your reputation grows as the community grows and anyone new entering the community to compete with the trusted advisor in that niche finds it almost impossible.

Crass and ineffective marketers crash their way into these online groups and communities, thinking they can self-promote, advertise heavily and sell products. It seldom works. The trusted advisor almost always wins.

The key is to connect and engage with these various communities, contribute to them, add value and create harmony.

When you find different groups in different places servicing the same community, you can choose to take part in one, several or all the groups.

It does take time, but can pay huge dividends, especially if you can re-use some of your advice in different groups and cross-fertilize between groups.

Your business can thrive in the online community by your valuable participation, not by the use or abuse of your marketing muscles.

Trends Closely Related to Communities

When you think about Communities, also think of these trends working in harmony with it:

Trend 4: Transaction Speed
Trend 9: Personal Connectivity
Trend 11: Linked Corporate Ecosystems
Trend 15: Globalization
Trend 16: 100% Perfect Fit Products
Trend 17: 1 to 1 Marketing
Trend 21: Popular Mass Culture
Trend 22: Trusted Brands
Trend 23: Peer Recommendations
Trend 25: Consumer Power

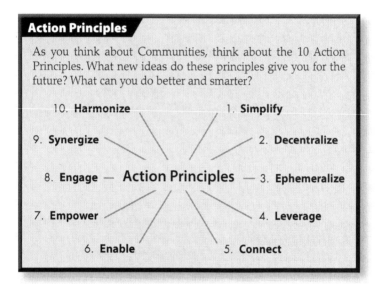

Action Principles

As you think about Communities, think about the 10 Action Principles. What new ideas do these principles give you for the future? What can you do better and smarter?

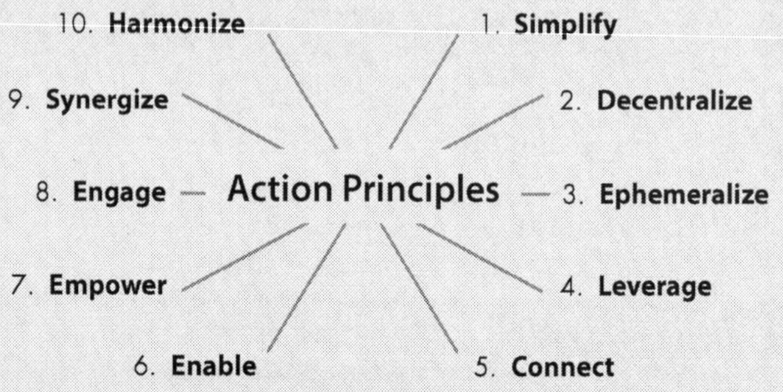

Some Questions To Ponder

1. What special interest groups or communities are your customers likely to belong to online?

2. Where do your customers go online? How can you find out?

3. What questions do your customers ask others online when they ask for help or advice?

4. Who is currently answering these online questions from your customers?

5. Who is currently the most trusted advisor for your customers?

6. How can you become the 'trusted advisor' for new prospective customers in their online communities?

Trend 11: Linked Corporate Ecosystems

- Increasingly greater interlinking of manufacturers, suppliers, vendors, customers and affiliates.
- Collaboration for mutual profit.
- Value Chains require Trust Chains.

In the online world, powerful business synergies come from collaborating in harmony with other businesses.

Collaborating online in trusted relationships with other businesses at different levels in your sales and supply chains creates your online ecosystem. Your online ecosystem gives your business extra capabilities, leverage and resources.

These linked participants add value to each other and can all profit from the tighter integration within the ecosystem.

Ecosystems vary, with some being loose partnerships or referral relationships.

Online retailers are setting up extended networks of sales affiliates who act as online commission-based sales agents for retail businesses.

Many manufacturers drive the formation of the ecosystem to support the production, distribution and sales of their products.

Businesses in highly linked and tightly integrated ecosystems can achieve substantial benefits from integrating information systems, inventory management systems, product manufacturing systems, databases and other business processes.

> ***Trust is the important glue***

Whether the ecosystem member is a manufacturer, supplier, distributor, vendor, customer or a sales affiliate, each player adds different value to the sales and supply chain.

Working together more closely brings synergistic benefits. The sales, marketing, customer support and production bonds become tighter from cooperation and collaboration.

Customer-supplier relationships are strengthened and both parties become more dependent and reliant on each other. Some choose to become locked-in to each other as a result of the mutual value provided and delivered.

Trust is the important glue required between all participants, and managing trust is one of the biggest issues within the online ecosystem.

Managing the access and sharing of data between businesses in the ecosystem is often challenging, especially if it is to be automated. Planning open, integratable and yet secure systems is important.

Plan For Long Marriage And For Easy Divorce

If you are a potential ecosystem member, think carefully before choosing to link up with other organizations.

Before you agree to integrate your systems with others, make sure you think about how you can quickly get out of the relationship if and when you need to.

It may seem unnecessarily pessimistic to devote time at the start to plan how you can extricate yourself if things don't work out, but do it anyway, no matter how unpopular it makes you.

You may stay happy and prospering in the ecosystem for years, but equally you may not. You need to be able to separate quickly without damaging your business.

Stay Flexible

To start with, tying your organization to others should be done in ways that loosely bind you but don't lock you in forever.

A rising tide may lift all ships in the ecosystem, but don't tie yourself too tightly to a leaky boat!

> ***You may need to separate quickly without damaging your business***

It's important to clearly define expectations and responsibilities at the start of the relationships. The ecosystem will prosper or fail on the value each member provides, the productive synergies each obtains and the strength of the trust that glues everyone together.

Trends Closely Related to Linked Corporate Ecosystems

When you think about Linked Corporate Ecosystems, also think of these trends working in harmony with it:

Trend 2: Internet Always On

Trend 3: 24.7 On-Demand

Trend 4: Transaction Speed

Trend 8: Technical Connectivity

Trend 9: Personal Connectivity

Trend 10: Niche Communities

Trend 12: Disintermediation

Trend 13: Transformation

Trend 18: Information Aggregation

Trend 19: Physical Location

Trend 22: Trusted Brands

Trend 24: Identity Control

Trend 25: Consumer Power

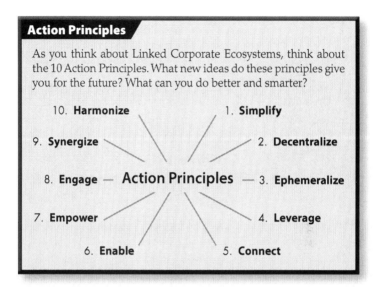

Action Principles

As you think about Linked Corporate Ecosystems, think about the 10 Action Principles. What new ideas do these principles give you for the future? What can you do better and smarter?

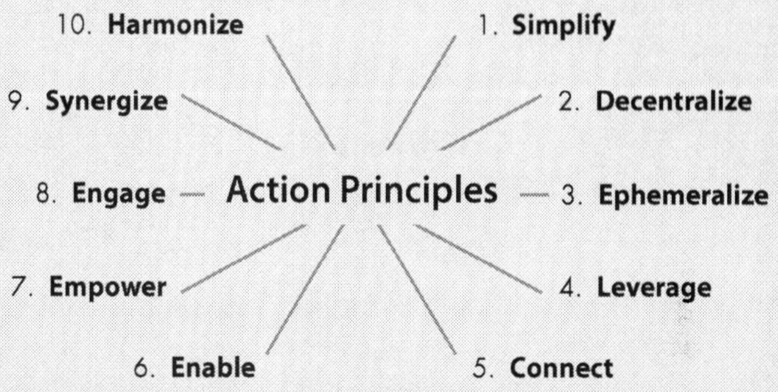

Some Questions To Ponder

1. What online ecosystems do your customers belong to already?

2. What ecosystems could your customers and suppliers join? How could this impact on you?

3. What ecosystems could you join or create to strengthen your business?

Trend 12: Disintermediation

- Middle-Men continue to be redefined and/or eliminated.
- Middle-Men must add more value with less cost, less friction, operate at higher speed and with greater efficiency.
- Middle-Men re-invent by adding more value or disappear!

Online, virtually anyone can connect with anyone else.

Given the opportunity, many end user customers would like to deal direct with producers or manufacturers in order to get fresher, newer, more relevant or cheaper products.

Many producers and manufacturers are happy to sell direct to end user customers if they can, rather than go through middle-men whose value-add is questionable or non-existent.

These Middle-Men businesses or Intermediaries are being threatened and challenged like never before. Many are being cut-out of sales and distribution channels. They are being'disintermediated'.

As soon as a producer or manufacturer can figure out how to efficiently make enough direct sales in smaller quantities to end-user customers, the old traditional distribution channel becomes redundant unless its various intermediary players add some value in the process.

Some middle-men who are not being elimir
having their roles reduced or redefined. Others are taking the initiative, and re-inventing their own role so they add more value in their supply, sales and distribution channels.

The old traditional channels offered value to each participant with economies of scale, volume purchasing, warehousing and trade finance.

Wholesalers and retailers typically use trade credit from their upstream distributors to fund their businesses, but distributors and manufacturers quickly become unhappy when they get paid slowly.

Poor sales and customer service from struggling retailers combined with disloyal wholesalers who are slow to move stock add to the frustrations of manufacturers.

Given the chance to deal direct with end user customers, many manufacturers are tempted to find a way to try out 'factory direct' sales.

One of the barriers to factory direct sales is the factory's desire to efficiently sell their products in large volumes rather than in the much smaller quantities requested by the typical end-user customer.

This volume purchasing has been the traditional 'value-add' of distributors and wholesalers, but now new middle-men are emerging to specifically handle warehousing, fulfillment and shipping logistics of 'factory-direct' physical products sold online on behalf of manufacturers.

Drop-shipping is an increasingly popular technique used by online retailers who take orders for products and automatically pass the orders onto drop-shipping businesses or manufacturers. These businesses fulfill the order, packaging the product and shipping it directly to the end customer on behalf of the retailer.

Even Manufacturers Get Disintermediated

Disintermediation can happen at any stage in a supply or sales chain. It can even happen at every stage, and at any stage. Even manufacturers of products are not safe, especially when they are manufacturing products designed by someone else.

New 3D personal printers are now entering the business and home consumer market. These printers allow 3 dimensional solid objects to be produced on demand using the printer.

Small home 3D printers may produce small plastic components, whereas larger 3D printers work with a range of materials.

Manufacturers and retailers and all the middle-men in between now face being disintermediated. Designers can sell their designs directly to consumers and provide the consumer with a digital file containing instructions for the 3D printer.

In 2011, The Economist magazine wrote *"Three-dimensional printing makes it as cheap to create single items as it is to produce thousands and thus undermines economies of scale. It may have as profound an impact on the world as the coming of the factory did....Just as nobody could have predicted the impact of the steam engine in 1750—or the printing press in*

1450, or the transistor in 1950—it is impossible to foresee the long-term impact of 3D printing. But the technology is coming, and it is likely to disrupt every field it touches."

Travel Industry

Look at the travel industry over the past 15 years and see Disintermediation at work, changing the sales processes of selling airline tickets, hotel rooms and more.

Low-cost carriers (LCC) in the airline industry base their sales channel on streamlined web-based bookings.

Intermediaries that add no value have been eliminated, but those that can add value are re-defining their strengths, and staying relevant in the industry.

Many travel agents have lost a revenue stream from basic ticket sales because they no longer need to do the seemingly mundane task of booking simple flights or accommodation.

We can book these tickets online ourselves now, and we take this for granted already, but jumping – or flying – into the unknown world of international travel is still risky for many people.

Travel agents can add their value by giving customers great advice and peace of mind in booking complex connecting flights or detailed holiday packages.

The travel agent's role as an expert in their field can allow them to re-define themselves, re-invent their point of difference in the marketplace, and re-build their brand as a reliable source of trusted information and specialist services.

New Middle-Men Are Appearing

New middle-men are appearing who can find the pain of their target customers, understand the problems and cleverly structure solutions that add value.

New middle-men are getting smarter, often with fully online business operations.

In the hotel and accommodation market, you can make an online booking directly with a hotel or resort, but hotels typically like to charge walk-in customers a high rack rate price, without any discounts. As an online customer you find yourself wondering if you are getting the best deal.

Comparison sites like HotelComparison.com and BellHop.com.au allow you to search for online deals.

Sites such as LastMinute.com and WotIf.com help travelers looking for cheap or available hotel rooms at short notice. Hotels enter their discounted prices for rooms that would otherwise probably be vacant. It's a win-win.

Other new intermediaries include Group purchasing sites such as Groupon and Scoopon which provide high volume discount deals to groups of consumers on behalf of manufacturers and other businesses. Time will tell about the sustainable value these group purchasing businesses add to the suppliers they represent.

Not all middle-men will die, but the roles of many middle-men are being re-defined to ensure they add more value with less cost, less friction, operate at higher speed and with greater efficiency.

To stay ahead of the game in your industry, look for opportunities to add more value in supply and sales processes.

Disintermediation is happening all around us in every industry. Lead it, follow it or get out of the way of it!

Trends Closely Related to Disintermediation

When you think about Disintermediation, also think of these trends working in harmony with it:

Trend 3: 24.7 On-Demand

Trend 4: Transaction Speed

Trend 7: Convergence

Trend 8: Technical Connectivity

Trend 9: Personal Connectivity

Trend 11: Linked Corporate Ecosystems

Trend 15: Globalization

Trend 16: 100% Perfect Fit Products

Trend 17: 1 to 1 Marketing

Trend 18: Information Aggregation

Trend 22: Trusted Brands

Trend 23: Peer Recommendations

Trend 25: Consumer Power

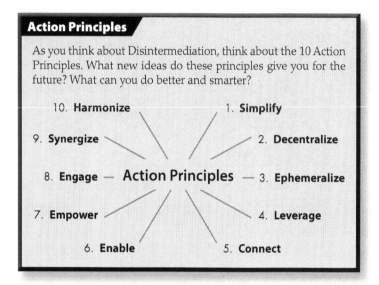

Action Principles

As you think about Disintermediation, think about the 10 Action Principles. What new ideas do these principles give you for the future? What can you do better and smarter?

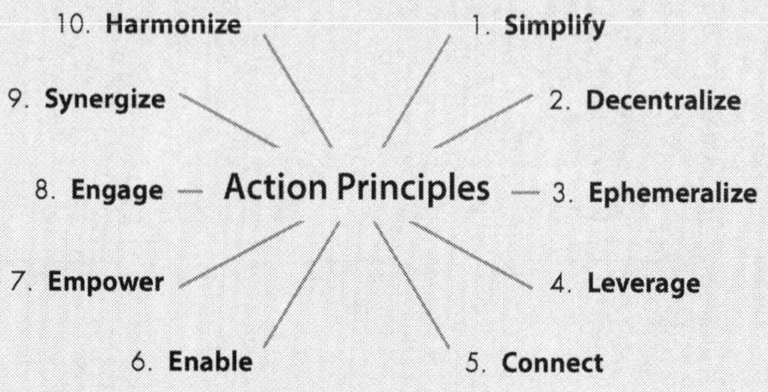

Some Questions To Ponder

1. Where do you fit in your sales and supply channels? How much control do you have?

2. Where are the points of friction and inefficiencies in your channels? How can you help to remove, reduce or re-define these impacts?

3. Would your suppliers be better off or worse off if you were not in the channel? What benefits and value would your suppliers not enjoy?

4. Would your customers be better off or worse off if you were not in the channel? What benefits and value would your customers not enjoy?

5. What could a smart new intermediary do to connect manufacturers to end-customers in your industry? What impact would that have on you?

Trend 13: Transformation (Atoms to Bits)

- Transformation of processes & products.
- Bits allow immediate online access and online delivery.
- The End-User pays for conversion to atoms.

Expensive and scarce atom-based physical products are being increasingly transformed into digital products made of bits of data.

Anything printed on paper such as newsletters, brochures, magazines, books and newspapers has either been digitally transformed already or probably will be in the future.

Digital transformation is not just about products. Processes are being transformed for the digital world.

These transformations have been happening for the past 15 to 20 years, and are going to continue.

Don't assume that because this is such an obvious trend, you no longer have to think about it. This is a key driver of change online and despite the transformation so far, it's still early days.

Simply transforming something from paper to digital does not make it smarter.

Smarter transformation adds value by enhancing the products and processes, and that's the exciting challenge for the future.

Digital Transformation

In a downloadable world, anything that can be transformed and digitized probably will be, especially if and when the transformation can add value by enhanced functionality and faster, easier, lower cost delivery to you online.

With downloadable music and video files, sales of compact discs have rapidly plummeted and DVD sales are set to become a thing of the past.

Atom-based products are expensive to produce, whereas bits can be produced and re-produced simply by creating and copying a computer file.

Physical products have mass and volume, and are expensive to store. Digital products can be stored anywhere. When digitized, your book collection can fit on a storage device the size of your thumb and your entire music collection can live inside your phone – making it more portable, more searchable and more convenient.

Distributing and shipping physical products is expensive and time-consuming. In the globally connected online world, digital products can be distributed anywhere anytime in seconds, and for little cost.

In case you're wondering, Catching Digital is available as both a printed book and as a digital ebook. Both formats have their strengths...

Bits Are Abundant

There is no scarcity with digital products, only abundance. It's core to the growth of the digital world.

Borrow an atom-based physically printed paper book from a library shelf and a gap appears on the shelf. No one else can borrow the same book at the same time.

Borrow a digital book from a digital library shelf, and there is no gap, no scarcity. The digital book can be borrowed or bought by other people at the same time.

The limitations on digital abundance come from the capabilities of computer servers, software and Internet connections but this is usually easily scalable.

Transforming Processes

Transformation applies to processes as well, not just products.

Try to buy a ticket for a flight, concert or sporting event, and chances are you will buy it online. The ticket will probably be sent to you in a PDF file that you can print out or it may be sent to your smartphone so it can be scanned on entry in a fully paperless digital process.

It's often easier, faster and more convenient for you to buy online, and it's faster, more convenient and cheaper for the ticket sales provider as well, even though some like to charge you a 'processing fee'.

Every time you fill in a form on a piece of paper, think how more efficiently the form could work if it was electronic and online. Surveys, courier receipts, medical forms, the list goes on.

Any paper-based form can be, and probably will be, digitally transformed. It will be produced, completed, stored and analyzed in a digital format.

> ***Transform your processes, not just your products***

Internally-Focused Process Transformation

Digital transformation is not just about converting paper to bits. Within organizations, manual processes involving humans doing repetitive tasks are being transformed and digitally enhanced.

As an example, table wait-staff in some smart restaurants no longer write food orders on paper order pads and take the order pad to the kitchen. They complete the order on a handheld device similar to a smartphone, and the order immediately appears on a display for the kitchen staff.

For the restaurant, it's not just about a better ordering system for the waiter. Keeping the whole process digital means the potential for better tracking and reporting of sales and products, improved inventory analysis, easier financial management and a whole lot more.

Customer-Focused Process Transformation

Look to your customers for ideas about process transformation. Think how improving your processes can make life better and more convenient for your customers.

Smart coffee shops are now receiving coffee orders from customers who use the shop's smartphone app to place an order so the customer no longer has to wait in a queue in the shop.

The customer's coffee is ready for them when they arrive which is more convenient for the customer and makes them feel special.

The app could also track purchases and integrate with the coffee shop's customer loyalty program to easily give bonuses to the customer.

Add in the ability for the coffee shop to pro-actively message the customer when they are nearby and the humble coffee shop can drive more sales rather than just waiting for them.

> ***Look to your customers for ideas. Remove pain, reduce friction, increase convenience.***

Risk Versus Investment

Global businesses can usually justify the costs of transforming product and process improvements, but it can be prohibitive for many small local businesses.

Local businesses will need to find cost-effective ways to transform their products and processes to remain competitive. Highly specific niche solutions will emerge for transforming process management in local businesses.

From scarce and slow moving atoms to abundant and rapidly moving bits, we've come a long way already. Enhancing products and processes through digital transformation is an ongoing game in the Digital Age.

Trends Closely Related to Transformation

When you think about Transformation, also think of these trends working in harmony with it:

Trend 3: 24.7 On-Demand

Trend 4: Transaction Speed

Trend 7: Convergence

Trend 11: Linked Corporate Ecosystems

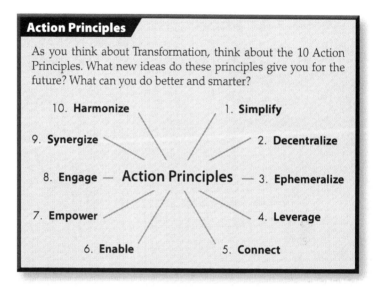

Action Principles

As you think about Transformation, think about the 10 Action Principles. What new ideas do these principles give you for the future? What can you do better and smarter?

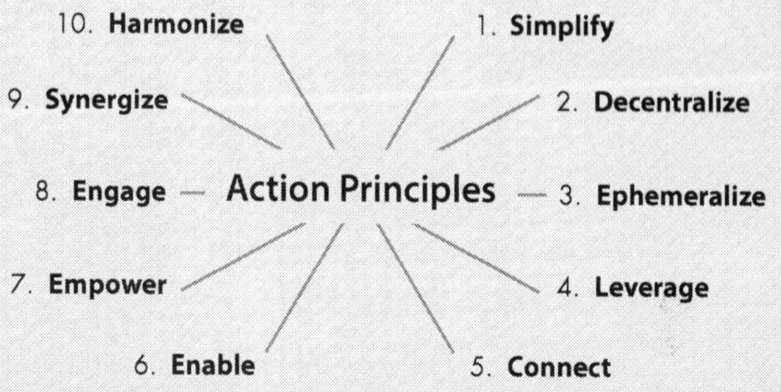

Some Questions To Ponder

1. What products and processes have you already transformed from 'atoms' to 'bits' to deliver online?

2. How do you still use paper in your business?

3. How can you transform and digitally enhance your products to add more value to them?

4. What processes could you transform and make more convenient for your customers?

5. Do you think the 'paperless office' is possible? When do you think it could happen in your business?

Trend 14: Mass Customization

- More customers can get exactly what they need & want.
- Cleverly custom-built products and services.
- Tailor-Made on a mass scale.

Production processes have changed over the years. Before the days of mass-production, many products were tailor-made. Products were custom-built as needed and made to order for each specific customer.

Being made to order meant that the preferences and choices of each customer could be accommodated and included in the product.

In theory, this approach would give the customer what they wanted and provide high levels of customer satisfaction. Things were made as needed, which meant the seller didn't have a lot of stock on hand waiting to be sold.

But there was a down-side. Production was often slow and expensive for the manufacturer. It was hard to achieve economies of scale if larger quantities of products were ordered.

"Any Color As Long As It Is Black"

In the 1920s, Henry Ford and others changed the concept of production of cars and in time, most other products as well.

Henry Ford famously said, "You can have any color you want as long as it is black." So, Ford's cars were black, for everyone.

Mass production of these standard cars allowed them to be produced faster and sold at far lower cost than custom-built cars which could not compete.

Mass production became the standard approach for most manufacturing processes. Product components were made separately in advance, and the product was assembled by specialists on an assembly line.

Not every product was black, but choices and options were limited. Changing the assembly line was time-consuming so the production line kept going, churning out products that may or may not be right for individual customers. Now we're in the Digital Age. We have smarter production equipment and connected customers.

"Any Parts & Any Color. You Choose"

In the Digital Age, the preferences of individual customers can be fed into smarter automated processes in smarter automated production equipment.

Now we can have individual products customized to suit individual customers, and produced cost-effectively on a mass scale. That's mass customization, and it's an increasing trend for the future.

Mass customization is happening in different industries, and sometimes by stealth. Levi mass customizes jeans, Adidas mass-customizes shoes, Bivolino mass-customizes dress shirts, and Reflect.com makes personalized beauty products based on the customer's skin type, age, and other variables.

Designs Mass Customized for 3D Printers

3 Dimensional Printers (as mentioned in the Trend 12 Disintermediation section) allow for manufacturing production processes to be done by the end user on the 3D printer in their home or office.

Instructions are sent to the 3D printer to tell the printer exactly what to produce, and in what size and colors.

Digital files sent to end-user customers by the designers of 3D products could easily be mass-customized with personalized printing specifications for individual customers.

Computers, Built To Order

Dell Computers doesn't hold stocks of pre-built computers that may or may not sell. Dell holds stocks of components and then builds computers as and when orders are received on the Dell website. These computers are delivered directly to customers, worldwide.

Dell holds minimal stocks of components. It operates on a Just In Time stock management basis so its inventories are low, keeping costs down and more importantly, reducing the likelihood of Dell holding large stocks of obsolete computer parts.

Change Your Retail Store, Instantly

Amazon uses mass-customization to automatically present different products on its website for different visitors based on their profile and purchase history.

Could a traditional bookstore or other retail shop set up displays of products in the store specifically to attract an individual customer the instant they walk in to the store? It would be pretty tricky, if not impossible to do in the offline world, and yet online Amazon does it with relative ease every day for its customers.

Amazon has over 2 million visitors to its website every day, and potentially each customer can see and buy specific products relevant to them.

Add in the tracking through the site and helping customers by making recommendations of what other similar people bought, and even the whole shopping experience becomes very customized – and on a mass scale.

Mass customizing of digital products such as software and music compilations can be an even easier process, but it's not just products that can be mass-customized for individual customers. Service based businesses also use the concept.

The Ritz-Carlton Hotel

The Ritz-Carlton hotel chain uses smart software to store information on customer preferences in a database so they can then personalize the customer's experience during their stay.

Unusual profile details are kept such as the guest's pillow choice, favorite newspaper, flowers or whether they like extra towels.

The hotel changes the hotel room for the customer before the customer arrives, making the room feel 'just right' for each individual guest.

The ability to mass customize products and services for individual customers can change whole industries. It can make customers love you and that can become a competitive point of difference.

It's about using digital technology to create a perfect fit for every individual customer. You can make everything 'just right'. It's a powerful trend in the Digital Age.

Trends Closely Related to Mass Customization

When you think about Mass Customization, also think of these trends working in harmony with it:

Trend 3: 24.7 On-Demand

Trend 16: 100% Perfect Fit Products

Trend 17: 1 to 1 Marketing

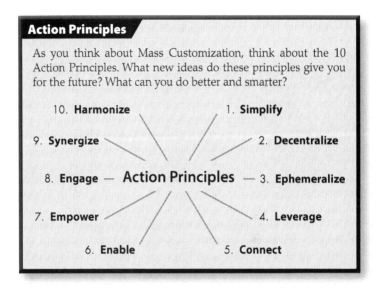

Action Principles

As you think about Mass Customization, think about the 10 Action Principles. What new ideas do these principles give you for the future? What can you do better and smarter?

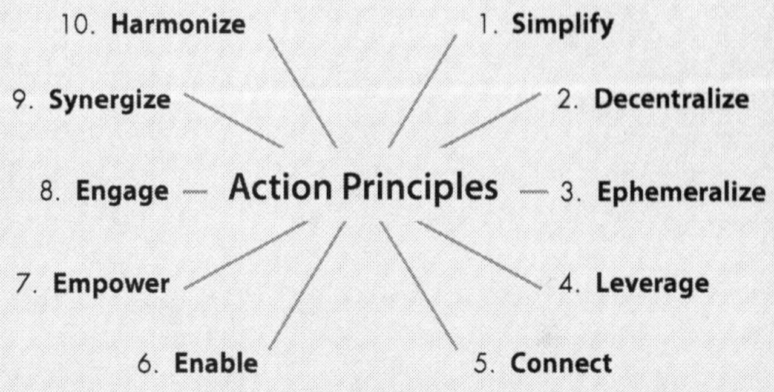

Some Questions To Ponder

1. How do you differentiate your products and services for different customers?

2. How do you give people more of exactly what they want, and less of what they don't want?

3. How could you change your sales, production or delivery processes to give individual customers a customized product or experience?

Trend 15: Globalization

- Increasing world markets.
- Increasing world competition.
- Increasing world standardization.

In a globally connected world, it may seem obvious we can now do business globally. What does that actually mean for business? What are the implications for you?

We now have the ability to more easily promote our own businesses globally online and be found online by prospective customers, wherever they are in the world.

We also have the ability to enter these world markets as customers, finding and buying products and services from anywhere in the world.

No Safe Backyard

We can buy globally, but so can our customers. Any business can face competition from another business anywhere in the world.

Gone is the safe territory of our own local backyard where we could reign supreme in our own local patch.

Now we have new competitors potentially attacking us and chasing our best customers.

We may not even know it is happening, let alone who these new competitors are. If we don't know, how we can defend ourselves?

New Product Benchmarks

New products will be developed for specific purposes and specific niches, but they'll be sold globally. Target customers will find these niche produces 'just right' which will make the products very easy to sell and very easy to buy.

These new products will set new standards and benchmarks for competitors.

It will no longer be possible, tolerable or acceptable for an inferior and more expensive product to dominate a local market purely on the basis of it being a locally made product.

Product standards will be driven higher, with more product features being provided at a lower cost.

In some cases, product standards may appear to drop as lowest common denominator products will be produced that are worse than what we currently have.

These will only succeed in the market is the quality is still acceptable and they are far cheaper to produce, sell, deliver and buy.

New Global Pricing Models

Prices will typically be driven lower by global competition. Businesses that previously used differential pricing models to sell the same products at different pricing levels in different geographic markets will have to re-think their pricing strategies for a more standard approach, often at a lower price.

One of the characteristics of digital products is that the location of the customer user can be tracked. Digital products can be disabled remotely if they are used in different geographic areas or jurisdictions that were not allowed for at the time of purchase.

Software companies and other digital product vendors have the ability to retain differential pricing models for different countries.

Vendors of physical products are more likely to see standard pricing models globally as customers shop around for the best deal on standard products.

Globalized Labor

Globalization makes more products and services appear to be generic. Skilled labor from knowledge workers can appear a commodity, but it varies greatly.

Skills, knowledge, initiative and creative ability are more related to the individual worker than the country in which they live.

Education, training, communication skills, culture and time-zone differences between countries add to the challenges of hiring labor in different countries.

Whether it be programmers, designers, researchers or other skilled technical people, comparing people with the same education qualifications and assuming they have the same skills and abilities is going to backfire on you.

In this globally connected world, it is inevitable that some businesses will add to their teams with skilled labor hired off-shore.

It is happening already, and we'll see more of it. New middle-men 'labor-hire' businesses are being set up to facilitate the hiring and employment processes.

It's easy enough to find off-shore specialists through sites like oDesk.com, vWorker.com, Freelancer.com, Elance.com and others.

oDesk supplies contractors using the system with software that automatically takes a snap-shot of their computer screen every 10 minutes and records the number of keystrokes the person makes in the time to determine their activity. This information is provided to the employer in an online Work Diary report.

You can also check out sites such as Amazon Mechanical Turk and Fiverr.com that allow outsourcing of very small tasks for small amounts of money.

As an example, the business model of Fiverr.com is based on tasks being done for USD $5.

Off-Shore Labor May Not Be 'Cheap' Labor

It's important not to think that off-shore labor means 'cheap' labor, although you can usually find people at lower costs in so-called third world countries than in many expensive Western-world cities.

See past the price, and see the abundance of people with skills. Off-shore labor usually means the availability of 'more' labor; more available and more accessible.

> ***See past the price, and see the abundance of people with skills.***

Simple supply and demand economics may lead you to think that the price of skilled labor off-shore will be lower than in your home town but that is not always the case.

Increasingly, these good, highly skilled off-shore-based knowledge worker laborers are learning and understanding their value in the global marketplace.

The workers are charging more and are being offered more. They are gravitating towards the best and most reliable employers.

Building The Best Teams

It's not surprising that the best workers want to work with the best employers and be part of the best teams. This is often the same in small local off-line businesses.

Imagine the power of it on a global scale online!

Niche service businesses with the Best Teams developing local and global reputations for offering best-of-breed near-perfect services to grateful customers who refer on their friends... It can be a powerful model.

Scalability to quickly grow the Best Teams is critical – and is available.

Add the ability to hire employees for the teams and have them operating in staggered time-zones around the world so the business can provide services 24.7 at times needed by its customers.

Sure, you might employ people at lower cost off-shore, but that's not the driver for the Best Teams. The best firms will prefer to employ the best talent they can find at prices they can afford to pay.

Larger pools of reliable skilled labor may reduce the price of labor, but the real strength of globalized labor is greater scale for labor-intensive businesses and business processes.

New Business Opportunities

Larger scalability creates new business opportunities for smart entrepreneurs who can match availability of labor supply in one or more parts of the world to availability of customer demand in other parts of the world.

As an example, one small innovative Australian accounting firm now employs dozens of highly skilled and qualified bookkeepers and accountants in the Philippines.

The wages paid to these employees are similar to what would be paid at the low end of the salary range in Australia, but are high in Filipino terms. As a result, the business is able to attract and retain long-term employees in the Philippines with greater confidence than in Australia.

The accounting firm's target customers in Australia are the owners of small businesses who have been doing their accounts themselves and who want to out-source this task and free up their time.

Without the scalability and reliability provided by this off-shore talent pool, the Australian business could not grow to the extent being demanded of it by prospective customers.

For this firm, the scalability also allows the high startup investment of running the off-shore office to be amortized over a larger number of staff. This progressively lowers the overhead costs, helping the business to increase its competitiveness as it grows off-shore.

Globalization better allows the scalability in matching labor pools to variable global demand.

Obviously the effects, impacts and implications are far-reaching. The price of different types of skilled and unskilled labor may tend to equalize across the globally connected marketplace.

This will cause pleasure for some and obvious pain for others. Our local societies will continue to change. People looking for employment in the digital age will need to keep their skills up to date and relevant.

Thousands of jobs are already moving around the world, depending on the availability of skilled and unskilled labor.

New jobs are being created using low-cost off-shore labor in business models that could never exist without low-cost labor. In other cases, existing jobs are moving from high cost countries to low cost countries, many never to return.

It's part of the globalization trend that will seem to make sense for the businesses involved and for those employees and contractors with skills in demand. Others will increasingly see globalization of labor in the Digital Age as a threat to their livelihoods.

Labor may become a commodity in the Digital Age, but not if you need and want your team to have the ability to innovate and invent with creativity and initiative.

Staying Local is a Strategy

In this globalizing world, you may choose to focus on your local markets rather than trying to operate and sell globally.

It may be a smart approach, but remember your backyard is not safe. You have to actively defend it and protect it. You can use online systems to better service your local clients.

Maximizing the human-to-human relationships between you and your customers could become your secret strength in a globally competitive world.

Trends Closely Related to Globalization

When you think about Globalization, also think of these trends working in harmony with it:

Trend 10: Niche Communities
Trend 12: Disintermediation
Trend 16: 100% Perfect Fit Products
Trend 19: Physical Location
Trend 20: Low Cost Software & Cloud Computing
Trend 21: Popular Mass Culture
Trend 22: Trusted Brands
Trend 25: Consumer Power

Action Principles

As you think about Globalization, think about the 10 Action Principles. What new ideas do these principles give you for the future? What can you do better and smarter?

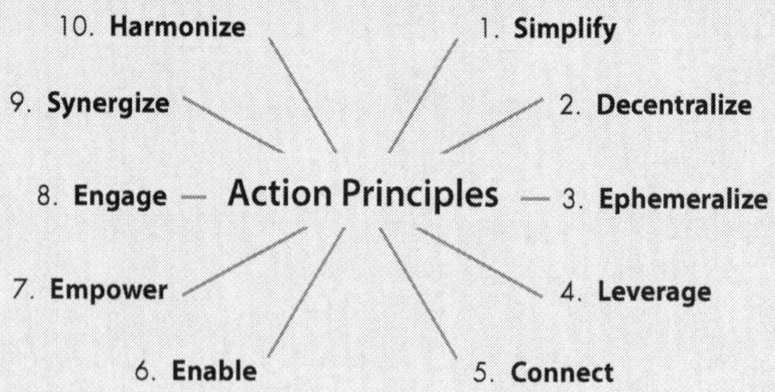

Some Questions To Ponder

1. How do your products and services compare with others available globally?

2. How much of your business comes from the local off-line world?

3. How safe are your sales territories?

4. Who is already trying to sell their products against you in your own back-yard? How do you know?

5. Which of your customers would move if offered a lower priced off-shore alternative to you? How many of your customers are already looking? How do you know?

6. If you run a people-intensive service business, how could you create one of the Best Teams in the world in your niche? What capabilities would this team need to have? What products and services could your offer? Would your customers be more attracted to you?

7. What would happen to your business is an existing or new competitor emerged with a Best Team in the world business and tried to attract your best customers?

Trend 16: 100% Perfect Fit Products

- Tightly defined niches can have tightly defined solutions.
- Increasing access to global scale makes 100% Niche solutions more viable, valuable and cost effective.
- Trusted suppliers can easily sell 100% fit solutions.

In the search to buy products and services for a specific need or requirement, customers often have to settle for something less than a perfect solution.

In the past, a good fit product may meet 80% of requirements. 80% is no longer good enough, especially when customers can find more and more 100% Perfect Fit solutions online.

Small Production Runs Are Not Viable Locally

Purchasing is usually a process of defining essential and desirable product features and requirements, then researching the market to see which Must-Have, Nice To Have and Non-Essential features are included or available in different products.

For customers, this shopping process generally involves compromises, with the perfect solution often hard or impossible to find.

Potential manufacturers of products and services in a small local niche market are often put off producing or even contemplating products that may be the perfect fit for a small handful of customers or a single customer.

Small run, small scale manufacturing is seldom viable and custom-building products for a single customer is usually prohibitively expensive and non-competitive.

Viable Scale in the Global Marketplace

Now with Internet, the manufacturer has access to the global marketplace. The specific needs and requirements of an individual customer in a tiny local niche may be identical to the needs of other customers in the same niche who live in other geographic areas around the world.

On this global scale, the question of viability and cost-effectiveness can change dramatically. A small non-viable local niche can become a very viable and profitable global niche.

The Perfect Solution

Entire new products and services can be produced which can be offered to these niche customers around the world. Sales won't be difficult as each customer will quickly recognize the perfect solution when they see it.

These customers will often pay a price premium to have the solution that is just right for them, and they are likely to become extremely loyal to the first provider of the '100% Perfect Fit' solution.

Any supplier who can demonstrate a sincere and deep understanding of the needs of a tightly defined niche of customers by developing a 100% solution to meet these needs will quickly establish a reputation that will be hard to compete against.

It can be cost-effective for one or even several small manufacturers or suppliers to sell 100% solutions into small global niches.

It's a good defense against large global manufacturers as the niche may appear a small and unattractive opportunity for these larger businesses looking for new markets in which they can easily compete and out-muscle smaller competitors.

"When it is possible to buy a 100% Perfect-Fit solution, trying to sell a 'good fit' solution will not be good enough."

The tighter a niche can be defined, the easier it becomes to identify and understand the needs of customers within the niche.

In a world in which it is possible to produce, sell, easily find and buy a 100% perfect-fit solution, trying to produce and sell a good fit solution may no longer be good enough.

Increasing access to global niche communities will result in an increasing understanding of the needs and wants of members of the niche community.

Attract the people in the niche, gain their trust, find out what they want and make products to meet their needs and wants.

Do this, and the products you make will virtually sell themselves.

Trends Closely Related to 100% Perfect Fit Products

When you think about 100% Perfect Fit Products, also think of these trends working in harmony with it:

Trend 10: Niche Communities

Trend 12: Disintermediation

Trend 14: Mass Customization

Trend 15: Globalization

Trend 17: 1 to 1 Marketing

Trend 20: Low Cost Software & Cloud Computing

Trend 22: Trusted Brands

Trend 23: Peer Recommendations

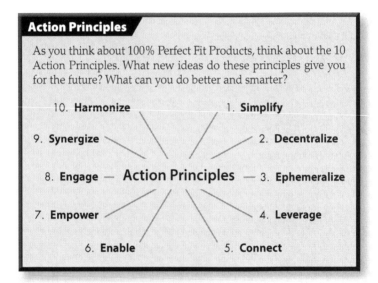

Action Principles

As you think about 100% Perfect Fit Products, think about the 10 Action Principles. What new ideas do these principles give you for the future? What can you do better and smarter?

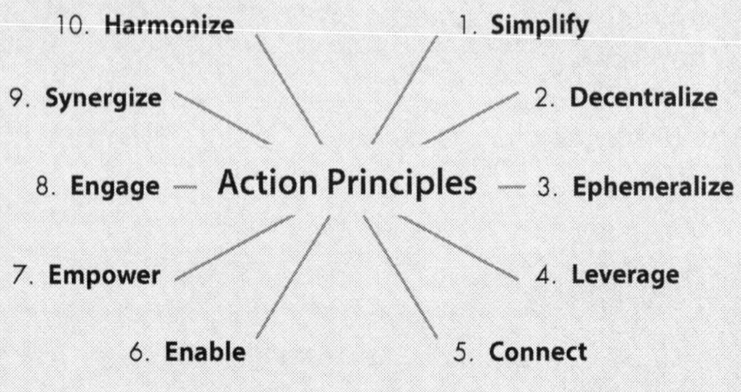

Some Questions To Ponder

1. How much business could you lose if your best customers were offered a 100% perfect fit solution by a competitor?

2. Who could be developing better 100% perfect fit products in your industry at the moment? How do you know? How can you find out?

3. What 100% perfect fit niche solution could you create and sell to others? Do you know how to produce, promote and provide it?

4. What 100% perfect fit solution would you like to buy and use in your business? Do you know where to find it?

Trend 17: 1 to 1 Marketing

- Marketing moving from the mass to the individual.
- Actions, responses & behaviors are trackable and accountable.
- Accurate customer databases and smart processes matter.
- Relationships still matter.

In the Digital Age, mass marketing is not smart marketing. Why would you treat everyone the same when you know they are different?

Why would you broadcast the same message to everyone? In the Digital Age, you can easily target specific messages to individuals, and you can do it on a mass scale.

You can personalize and customize each of the messages you target to thousands or millions of individuals at a lower cost with better results and more accountability than old-style mass marketing could achieve.

We're not talking about spam email. Spam has never been smart. 1 to 1 Marketing can use email to'push'messages to your customers and prospects, but a variety of other push/ pull marketing tools can be used to produce customizable messages and may be more effective than email.

Currently these include social media feeds and advertising, videos, interactive web apps, smart website ads, re-targeted web display ads, smart mobile apps, SMS message, tweets and , Twitter,

Smart 1 to 1 In Real Time

1 to 1 Marketing is not just about smarter individual advertising messages. Smart 1 to 1 Marketing can specifically target customers who are in the process of shopping and purchasing.

The innovative US-based firm, SteelHouse.com provides a behavioral-based commerce platform which gives marketers the ability to deliver targeted offers to specific shoppers in real time.

These offers are based on the shoppers' profile and buying behavior on the marketer's website, and it's all managed in real time.

Customer Relationship Management

1 to 1 Marketing requires more than just running a good Customer Relationship Management (CRM) system. Smart business is always about relationships, and building strong person-to-person relationships is the key.

You can use technology tools to help manage 1 to 1 relationships on a mass scale at both a local and global level. You have the ability to communicate with each customer as an individual

Many Businesses Get It Wrong

Sadly, many businesses still get it wrong. They don't engage effectively with customers, take the time or effort to learn techniques that are effective, find the right tools or get the right training.

They have multiple customer databases, don't keep their customer profiles up to date, and can't easily access a single view of the customer's history.

In a 1 to 1 environment, messages are not just personalized for individuals, but are relevant, timely and valuable. Messages that are not may never get noticed in the clutter and noise of your customers' daily lives.

Customer Service Costs Increase

Even with smart technology systems, managing 1 to 1 relationships with all of the individuals in your customer database will generally be more time-consuming than mass communicating with them.

Customer service costs will probably increase. Your Return On Investment (ROI) may not be immediately obvious.

Automation

More organizations are trying automated customer-facing processes to reduce costs of relationship servicing and better cope with global scale.

Automation needs to improve customer relationships and customer service levels rather than just reduce the costs for you to provide the service. Many businesses get this wrong which creates opportunities for competitors.

Trackability and Accountability

In the 1 to 1 Marketing world, almost everything about the customer is trackable and accountable.

You can track every click, every action and every reaction your customer makes on your website, emails and other Internet-based communication pieces.

You can target each individual customer with specific advertising messages and content and track the effectiveness at an individual level.

Analysis reports can be produced for every important stage in your sales funnel and pipeline.

This accountability will continue to be great for online advertising companies who can prove they deliver cost-effective results; and it will continue to threaten and destroy the less competitive and unaccountable traditional advertising sales media.

Trust is Key

Relationships are critical in 1 to 1 Marketing, and trust is the glue to good relationships. Trust is hard to build but easy to destroy.

Don't risk breaking trust by having a confused or careless approach to your marketing processes, your customer service, your databases or your handling of your customer's information.

Here's a question for you and your marketing team to always ask before you change a process, launch a new marketing campaign or communicate with your customers:

"Will this action enhance the level of trust our customer places in us or does it risk reducing trust?"

Trends Closely Related to 1 to 1 Marketing

When you think about 1 to 1 Marketing, also think of these trends working in harmony with it:

Trend 3: 24.7 On-Demand

Trend 4: Transaction Speed

Trend 8: Technical Connectivity

Trend 9: Personal Connectivity

Trend 10: Niche Communities

Trend 12: Disintermediation

Trend 14: Mass Customization

Trend 16: 100% Perfect Fit Products

Trend 18: Information Aggregation

Trend 19: Physical Location

Trend 20: Low Cost Software & Cloud Computing

Trend 22: Trusted Brands

Trend 23: Peer Recommendations

Trend 24: Identity Control

Trend 25: Consumer Power

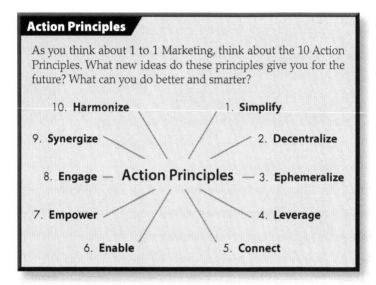

Action Principles

As you think about 1 to 1 Marketing, think about the 10 Action Principles. What new ideas do these principles give you for the future? What can you do better and smarter?

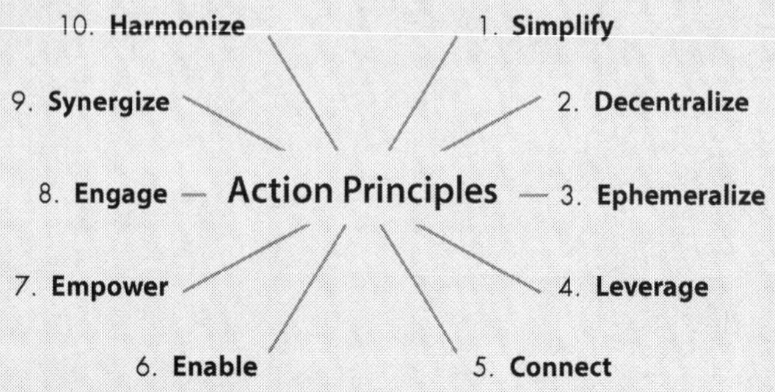

Some Questions To Ponder

1. What do you know about your customers? Is this knowledge stored in a database or is it stored in the heads of you and your team?

2. How accurate, up-to-date and comprehensive is your customer database?

3. How much of your marketing and advertising is to the masses? Why?

4. How good are your customer relationships? How do you know?

5. What aspects of your customers' behavior do you track? What would you like to track?

6. Could you use your customer database more effectively?

Trend 18: Aggregation of Information

- Information filtered by you or by an aggregator.
- More reliance on credible and trusted aggregators.
- Trusted information from trusted brands & trusted peers.
- Bias, censorship or just better search results?

Anyone can be a publisher in the online world and the web is collecting a lot of inaccurate, unhelpful and useless content.

Sifting through to find what is valuable and accurate is not easy and takes time.

Content aggregators play an increasingly important role in sourcing and filtering content on specific topics or niche areas.

These aggregators are web-based Middle-Men who add value for other users by saving time and finding, filtering and re-presenting the best content quickly.

Popular types of content being aggregated include news, reviews, blogs and videos.

News aggregators who select what news they pass on to users include The Huffington Post and the Drudge Report, whereas sites like Google News operate with automated processes.

Popular review aggregators include Metacritic, Rotten Tomatoes and Epinions. Examples of popular video aggregators are Dailymotion.com, Metacafe.com and Break.com.

The mobile app for Flipboard aggregates content from other publishers and re-formats it into an attractive and easy-to-read magazine style for tablet devices like the iPad.

"Finding aggregators you can trust to provide independent, unbiased and uncensored content will be increasingly important."

Aggregation software allows users to create their own content aggregation by subscribing to RSS syndicated content feeds. The software accesses the selected RSS content feeds and automatically presents the latest content for the user to view.

Similarly to traditional news or magazine publishers, online aggregators source, filter and select content based on their individual criteria.

Finding aggregators you can trust to provide independent, unbiased and uncensored content will be increasingly important.

Unlike the traditional model of publishing, every action users take to view and interact with this digital content can be tracked and recorded.

Every interaction with digital content can be tracked and recorded

This tracking can be helpful to allow the aggregator to fine-tune the delivery of more relevant content and relevant advertising messages, but it can create the potential for massive privacy issues.

The line between a Content Aggregator and a Search Engine is becoming increasingly blurred. For example, Google Maps aggregates location-related content and presents local content with a map interface.

Google, Bing and other search engines face the ongoing dilemma of how to select the content to show in search results, and they wield enormous market power in their selections.

Most publishers have the power to choose what they publish. Every editor makes decisions about what to include or reject.

Search engines wield enormous market power

Very few publishers make totally independent and unbiased choices. It's the same with content aggregators. What they find online and how they choose to filter and re-package defines the information you access online.

Trends Closely Related to Information Aggregation

When you think about Information Aggregation, also think of these trends working in harmony with it:

Trend 4: Transaction Speed

Trend 7: Convergence

Trend 8: Technical Connectivity

Trend 11: Linked Corporate Ecosystems

Trend 12: Disintermediation

Trend 17: 1 to 1 Marketing

Trend 21: Popular Mass Culture

Trend 22: Trusted Brands

Trend 23: Peer Recommendations

Trend 24: Identity Control

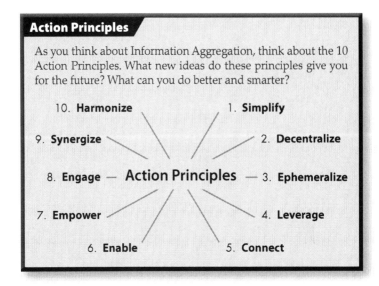

Action Principles

As you think about Information Aggregation, think about the 10 Action Principles. What new ideas do these principles give you for the future? What can you do better and smarter?

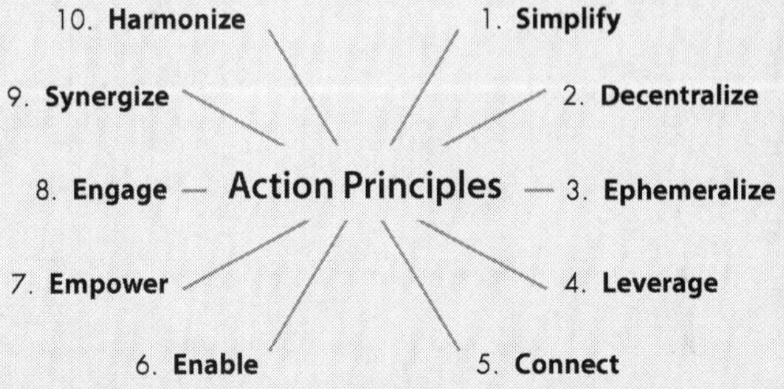

Some Questions To Ponder

1. What information do you provide to your customers and others online?

2. What information sources do your customers use?

3. Who do your customers trust to tell them what is really going on in your industry?

Trend 19: Physical Location

- Your physical location is increasingly LESS relevant to you.
- Your physical location is increasingly MORE relevant to others.
- Businesses selling physical products want to know where you are.
- Connected businesses can operate from anywhere.
- Connected people can work for anyone, anywhere.

With high speed wireless networks and smart mobile devices, more people can be effectively productive anywhere.

Businesses have less need for the fixed costs and constraints of a physical business office. Customers can make purchases while they are mobile and almost anywhere in the world.

It hasn't always been that way.

Your Location Is Less Relevant To You

As long as you are connected, you can operate from almost anywhere.

Knowledge workers who make their living on a computer can be located anywhere, as long as they are connected.

Productive mobility has reduced the need for a traditional office workplace, and replaced it with an office workspace.

In this new office workspace, your staff need the ability to concentrate free of distractions and use reliable tools and infrastructure.

They also need to be able to enjoy the positive social benefits of the old-style workplace and stay motivated as part of the team to achieve the business purpose.

Workspaces can be anywhere. We have more choices of how we work, where we work and often when we work.

We have more choices to select those we employ to work with us. With global connectivity comes the ability for any business to employ knowledge workers located in another country. Their time zone, communication skills and work skills may be important to you, but their location may not be. (See Trend 15 Globalization.)

> ***"Workspaces can be anywhere"***

Your Location is becoming More Relevant to Others

Your location may be less important for you, but it is becoming more important to businesses wanting to reach you, especially when you move near to their location.

Location tracking is embedded into smart phones, and almost every smart phone advertising applications will try to track your location.

Shopping centers are using proximity tracking of shoppers' smartphones to better understand the patterns and flow of traffic through the center.

If you know where your customers are and know when they come near your store, you can run use 'proximity marketing' and special sales promotions to encourage them to visit your business.

Special offers, bonuses and loyalty points are easier to provide and record on smartphone apps. (See Trend 6: Smart Mobile Devices.)

Foursquare is a social network platform in which users are encouraged to 'check-in' on the smartphone when they enter a local business that participates in Foursquare.

By checking-in, users let their friends know they are at the location, and users can collect a reward from the business for checking in and promoting that business to others.

"Smartphone marketing apps will try to track your location"

The tools are evolving, and location-based marketing is a rapidly growing area. One of the names currently given to the growth in this area is SoLoMo, the combining of Social Media, Local Marketing and Mobile location-based marketing services.

This is already proving to be important in areas such as tourism, hospitality and entertainment, with users of SoLoMo apps and sites being able to share their experiences through online check-ins, photos, videos, comments, reviews and updates.

Trends Closely Related to Location

When you think about Physical Location, also think of these trends working in harmony with it:

Trend 2: Internet Always On

Trend 3: 24.7 On-Demand

Trend 5: Fast Wireless Networks

Trend 6: Smart Mobile Devices

Trend 11: Linked Corporate Ecosystems

Trend 15: Globalization

Trend 17: 1 to 1 Marketing

Trend 24: Identity Control

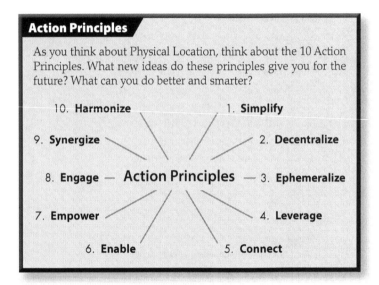

Action Principles

As you think about Physical Location, think about the 10 Action Principles. What new ideas do these principles give you for the future? What can you do better and smarter?

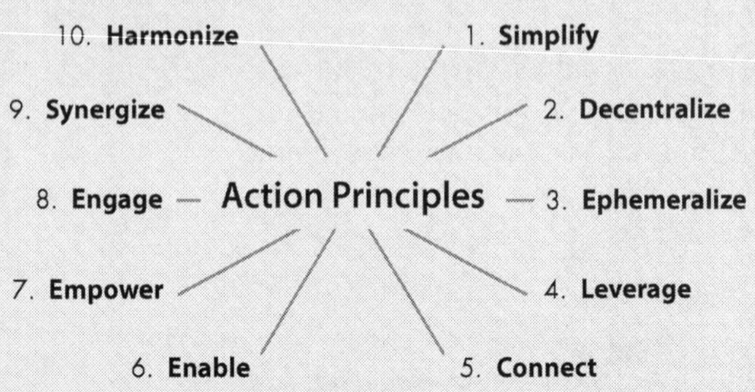

Some Questions To Ponder

1. Do you care about the location of your customers?
2. Do your customers care where you are?
3. Who else cares about the location of your customers?
4. What would your customers like to share with others about you? How are they doing this currently?

Trend 20: Low Cost Software & Cloud Computing

- Free or Low cost & extensible open source software.
- Low cost processing power and data storage facilities.
- Scalable low-cost hosted services platforms.
- Supported by communities of developers.
- Less software needs to be custom-built.

Almost every business has some type of computer software to assist in the operations of their business. Many businesses regularly use dozens of different software applications.

How will your business select its software in future?

The price of software is continually reducing and the functionality of the software typically increases. This means you get software that does more and costs less.

Sometimes the better software doesn't do more for you but it becomes more specific to meet your needs and the needs of other users just like you.

Better Software At Lower Costs

So, why can you now get much better software at a much lower cost? What's driving it?

New software programming tools are making programming faster, easier and simpler.

The Open Source software movement is growing. Complex software is being collaboratively developed by communities of enthusiasts around the world. Some Open Source products are very good and often distributed for free.

Custom-built software developed for a single customer is being released as low-cost products for global niche market segments in new 100% Perfect Fit software solutions. (See Trend 16.) This is raising the quality benchmarks and productivity in different industries.

Thanks to the Internet, software can be easily promoted, downloaded, tested and purchased globally with far less marketing and promotion costs for the software vendors.

Mobile applications (apps) can be developed for highly specific niche markets and purposes, and then rolled out to these markets globally through Apple's iTunes App Store or Google's Android Marketplace at little or no promotional cost.

Niche communities often provide links to their own software marketplaces, and sites like SourceForge provide repositories for downloadable software.

The high speed online connectivity allows software to be continually improved, and easily and automatically updated for customers.

Massive online storage capabilities provide new capacity for hosting software externally at a low cost.

The result is an increasingly high take up and adoption of software tools that are reliable, proven, scalable, low-cost and often free.

Many of these free or low cost web-based software applications are now available for home users, small business users and the corporate market segments.

Today and more so into the future, good low cost software can easily be extended in functionality and capability. (i.e. it is 'extensible').

Good software is also with other software products produced by other software developers. Integration is becoming increasingly easier with open systems and common protocols and database formats. To be successful, technical integration must be reliable, easy, scalable and secure.

Connecting to "The Cloud"

The Internet has long been referred to as a Cloud, and the concept of Cloud computing has grown in recent years.

In the Cloud computing world, software applications, customer data and related data storage are managed 'in the Cloud'.

Ideally, being 'in the Cloud' means being on a network of inter-connected servers located in highly secure data centers throughout the world, providing fail-safe redundancy and scalability at a low cost.

Other benefits offered by good Cloud computing firms are a well-managed and secure technical environment with high automation, flexible growth for the future, easy mobility for users, reduced costs and with lower risks.

It can free up your own organization to be able to use good IT systems without having to buy them, constantly upgrade them, keep them working and worry about them.

If that all sounds too good to be true, you're right. You probably won't have easy access to help when you need it, and it may end up not being the cheap, low-cost option you envisaged.

Many Cloud firms will not provide the levels of support you may be used to, especially if you have novices in your team or are not happy to support yourself by finding advice and technical answers in user forums and knowledge bases.

If the Cloud provider is located on the other side of the world and wants to have down-time for upgrades during the early hours of their morning, this could be in peak business times for you.

To make it worse, all Clouds are not the same.

Imposters In The Cloud

The Cloud computing industry has been evolving quickly, partially driven by reduced IT spending during the Global Financial Crisis years of 2007 to 2009.

It's attracted lots of IT businesses that have shifted their operations to the Cloud to cash in on the Cloud bandwagon.

Many so-called Cloud-based firms are imposters, who simply may have one or two servers connected to the Internet. The servers may be in some data center somewhere or may be located in someone's bedroom. (Yes, this still happens.)

The imposters sell cheap services to unsuspecting customers who buy based on low prices and the Cloud buzz-word. Obviously, businesses that use and trust these dodgy Cloud providers could be putting themselves at great risk.

These providers don't have the growth scalability nor the redundancy, back-up systems, security or skilled support you may assume.

> ***Many so-called Cloud-based firms are imposters***

Cloud computing has also been driven by consumers who use cloud-based applications on smart mobile devices and now expect and demand the same easy- to-use functionality, connectivity and efficiencies when at work.

Basing your judgment simply on how something works and how easy it is to use can make you overly trusting of the software and its providers.

With Cloud computing, many users do not know or even care what equipment or resources they are connecting to or where these systems are physically located.

This 'care-less' approach may be fine when you are using game programs or fun mobile apps that are not mission-critical, but for your business data – and your customers' business data – we business owners need to be care-full and not care-less. The information we hold on our customers and others needs to be protected and secured.

The very name 'Cloud' lulls us into thinking it is soft, pure, fluffy and even fun, but in reality your data is being managed and stored somewhere where you have no control.

Cloud data centers are big targets to hackers, and your data is potentially accessible to unauthorized intruders.

Software In The Cloud

In the world of Cloud Computing, you can now get to use software, hosting and storage infrastructure without buying it. You no longer need to find the physical space to house servers and them keep them securely running in your own office.

An increasing number of highly functional and scalable hosted software solutions are available for business use.

One of the current names for this concept is Software as a Service (SaaS). The providers of it may get called SaaS providers, Application Service Providers, Platform Service Providers or simply Cloud Providers, and yes, it can get a bit confusing.

IT companies add to the confusion by using the terms interchangeably or inventing new jargon in their scramble to define their own uniqueness.

One of the SaaS leaders is Salesforce.com. Here's how Salesforce currently describes itself on its website:

"As cloud computing providers, we offer CRM software as a service with our Force.com cloud computing platform, so that you can multitask and keep track of your customers and your budget at the same time - a must in today's economy. The world's best-loved Platform-as-a-Service can be working for you"...

SaaS is bought by customers on a month to month basis, usually with no license fees, no set up costs and no implementation time delays. The customers need no specialist technical expertise or servers or infrastructure.

The low-cost monthly fees can appear to be attractive for business customers who are only considering short-term usage, but SaaS fees paid monthly for many years can become very expensive compared to other options.

SaaS gives you cost savings from not needing to supply the infrastructure to host the software yourself. More importantly, you don't need to pay for your own technical experts to set it up and keep it working.

The apparent scalability of the typical SaaS solutions is impressive. Even if the sales-blurb claims of the SaaS providers are truthful and accurate, not all of them will be totally reliable, scalable and able to cope with their own possible massive success without crashing.

Selecting and then relying on a SaaS provider for your essential business processes should require more than just faith and blind trust.

Many businesses are taking unknown risks, often blindly.

Big SaaS & Cloud Risk: Your Data

An often unforeseen risk with Cloud-based services is in the retrieval of your data if and when you wish to terminate the use of the service.

Many online SaaS and Cloud services are easy to sign up to and even easy to cancel, but it can be difficult and sometimes impossible to get your data back in an easily useful format when you terminate the service.

This is an intentional tactic on the part of the provider, but often won't be disclosed to you anywhere but in the extremely fine print, which you may never have read.

Some SaaS companies try to claim ownership of your data. Others may give your data back to you, but only in some raw data format unreadable by you without access to other special software.

Your business probably has legal requirements to store business data for many years in case government agencies need to audit you.

In Australia, some data needs to be stored for seven years, and some training organizations need to keep data records for 30 years.

If you have to continue to pay a SaaS provider to keep your data just to meet your legal requirements, you could pay seven years of ongoing monthly fees.

Years of fees can be expensive, and even more so if you have already chosen to move off that particular hosted platform.

Privacy issues are also being raised. SaaS providers in other countries may be required to give their government full access to all of your data. This is usually the case with US-based SaaS providers, and many SaaS providers are located in the US.

You often will not be able to find out exactly where your data will be located. You also will never know who has access to it.

You need to assume that anyone who works for the SaaS provider could see your data, and you also need to assume that sooner or later your data may be hacked by someone outside the SaaS company.

There are security risks even with good Cloud providers, but good large Cloud operators can usually employ better security experts than any individual small business could afford.

Not all cloud computing providers are the same, and the ignorance or apathy of business customers looking for a cheap provider will expose them to risks and threats.

You need to be extra careful about data ownership and getting your data back in a readable form. If your data and your customers' data are stored somewhere in a cloud, you want to be careful it's not a storm cloud!

The Internet Growth Spiral

Despite these issues, growth of low cost software and storage solutions continues. Underpinning it all is, of course, the growth of the Internet.

There is a growing spiral effect. Improvements in hardware and connectivity inspire the development of more and better software which attracts more users. More users provide the business case to drive further improvements and add more capability, more powerful hardware and even better connectivity.

There is still a market for individually custom-built software to meet the specific requirements of unique individual customers, but it is a shrinking market.

Look for pre-built, low cost, open systems that can be extended and integrated to give you the functionality you need.

Don't just believe reviews you find online about software, vendors and providers. Many will be biased, and may be written by the vendors themselves or sales agents who will receive a sales commission for directing customers to the vendor.

Check independent reviews from trusted advisors and others you know and trust in your community.

Remember, 'Open' generally trumps 'Closed', and 'Integrated' will increasingly trump 'Fragmented'. There are more tips for choosing software later in this book.

Trends Closely Related to Low Cost Software & Cloud Computing

When you think about Low Cost Software & Cloud Computing, also think of these trends working in harmony with it:

Trend 1: Moore's Law
Trend 2: Internet Always On
Trend 4: Transaction Speed
Trend 5: Fast Wireless Networks
Trend 6: Smart Mobile Devices
Trend 8: Technical Connectivity
Trend 15: Globalization
Trend 16: 100% Perfect Fit Products
Trend 17: 1 to 1 Marketing
Trend 22: Trusted Brands
Trend 24: Identity Control

Action Principles

As you think about Low Cost Software solutions and Cloud Computing, think about the 10 Action Principles. What new ideas do these principles give you for the future? What can you do better and smarter?

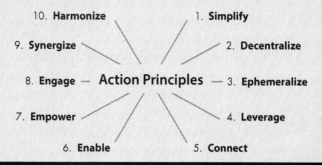

Action Principles

1. **Simplify**
2. **Decentralize**
3. **Ephemeralize**
4. **Leverage**
5. **Connect**
6. **Enable**
7. **Empower**
8. **Engage**
9. **Synergize**
10. **Harmonize**

Some Questions To Ponder

1. What Cloud-based software applications do you use at the moment? How good and trustworthy are your Cloud providers? Have you ever checked? Do you know how to check?

2. What data can you put in the Cloud? What data do you have that should not go into the Cloud?

3. Do your clients want their data put into the Cloud? How do you know?

4. What is the risk to your business if your Cloud-based data is hacked and stolen?

5. For how many of your software systems are you locked in to a specific software vendor? Are you happy with that?

6. Who has access to your data?

7. Who selects the software systems for your business?

8. Can you easily extend your systems and integrate with others?

9. Are your software systems low cost? Are they Closed or Open? Are they Fragmented or Integrated?

Trend 21: Popular Mass Culture

- Search engine results show 'popular' pages and sites.
- Sites like YouTube shows 'popular' videos.
- 'Popular' may not be 'right'.
- Marketing focuses on creating "swells" in popular culture that attract mass audiences.
- Beware the Vested Interests.

How do you find something online? Typically, most people are being increasingly exposed to what is 'popular' with others. This is not just technical and scientific information, but reaches into entertainment, the arts and culture.

Increasingly, search engine tools such as Google and Bing are showing us search results based on what is popular.

Facebook shows us newsfeeds based on what is popular; Twitter shows trending topics of what is popular and YouTube gives priority to videos that are popular.

How do you find something online if it is not popular? How do you know that something popular is also something accurate?

Something that is popular for others could be totally wrong or wrong for you.

The more that people are encouraged to view a popular item, the more they are likely to do so. The popularity of the item can then increase in a self-fulfilling positive feedback loop. It can become more popular, but it may still be wrong.

Beware The Vested Interests

It may seem helpful to have suggestions based on what other people find popular, but the basis of how the suggestion is being made to you needs to be understood, questioned and even challenged.

What vested interests are at work in making these suggestions?

You may never see or even realize that something is being pushed onto you. Often this pushing is not disclosed, but disguised as helpfulness. You are encouraged to think 'the system' is helping you.

> ***Creating the buzz is about creating the perception of popularity***

If something is popular with one group of people or even a mass of people online, it does not mean it will be popular for you or the groups to which you may belong.

Just because something is popular does not make it right or good. Popularity alone does not even make something worthwhile to be viewed; it may just be sensationalized, over-hyped, biased or attention-seeking.

Generating online hype and popularity is becoming part of deliberate business strategy.

Managing online product launches has become a big area of online sales and marketing. An important element is the creation of the'pre-launch buzz'throughout the target communities and niche markets.

Creating the buzz is about creating the perception of popularity.

If you see an advertisement for a new product you may simply ignore it, but if you receive messages about a new product from enough people in your niche or community, you are likely to pay attention.

That's how the buzz can be created.

It's not easy to know whether the new product is as great as everyone is saying until you try it, or until you read honest reviews from people you trust.

Initial product reviews may be biased and self-serving comments from affiliate marketers looking to receive a sales commission from product sales they generate.

Many people with vested interests working together online help to create online buzz. They count on the herd mentality driving sales. They talk of sales funnels, and as always,'sales'is a numbers game.

Popularity is a numbers game, but it also has emotion attached to it. The buzz can be made to look and feel exciting, valuable and worthwhile to you.

If you are aware of the techniques, you can start to question it.

Are you being remotely managed by smart marketers and being treated as part of the herd?

Or are you making a rational and independent critical purchasing decision?

Worse still, you may be being guided or seduced into following the herd and enhancing the popularity of something that could be unhelpful to you, sinister or even harmful. It happens; this is how some computer viruses are spread so rapidly online.

How Do You Create Popularity?

Creating product popularity has always been a marketing and advertising task, but now the tools have changed.

Specific tools and techniques are available to create online popularity, or at least the appearance of it.

As something online appears to become more popular, a cultural swell occurs which continues to grow through the positive feedback loop, attracting more of a mass audience.

Part of the marketing challenge is that the audience is not necessarily captive and looking for what you have to offer. You have to find them, or more likely in the online world, they have to find you.

> ***You may be seduced into following the herd***

The audience may be open and receptive to what you are offering or promoting, but you also need them to react and respond favorably to you.

Having your video clip go viral on Facebook or YouTube may need the recommendations of hundreds or thousands of people, or just one influential person in charge of a large Facebook group.

Your video could be given a listing in YouTube's top ten, with subsequent exposure to an audience of millions.

Something being recommended on the basis of its popularity may appear to be helpful to you, but remember, it's a commercial world and ultimately, money talks. The question is who is paying?

Trends Closely Related to Popular Mass Culture

When you think about Popular Mass Culture, also think of these trends working in harmony with it:

Trend 9: Personal Connectivity

Trend 10: Niche Communities

Trend 15: Globalization

Trend 18: Information Aggregation

Trend 22: Trusted Brands

Trend 23: Peer Recommendations

Trend 25: Consumer Power

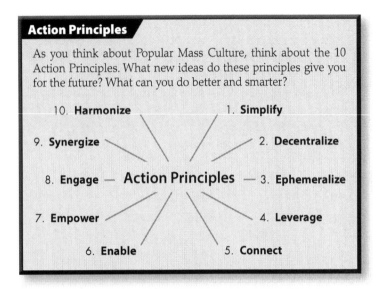

Action Principles

As you think about Popular Mass Culture, think about the 10 Action Principles. What new ideas do these principles give you for the future? What can you do better and smarter?

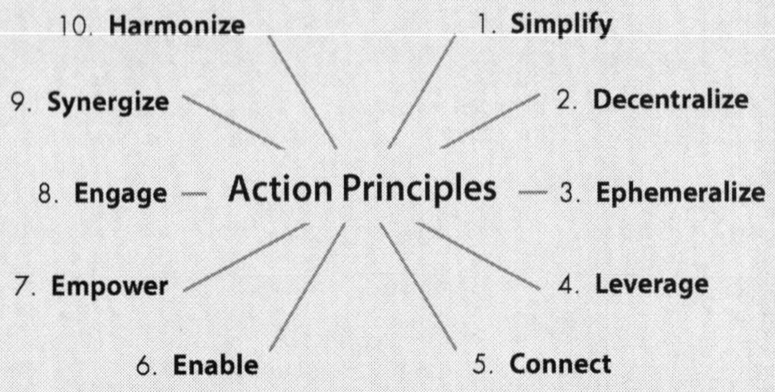

Some Questions To Ponder

1. How do you fit in to the 'Popular' world?

2. Is your business 'popular'?

3. What are your prospective customers typically looking for when they search online for a supplier such as you?

4. If they look for you, do they find you or do they find what is 'popular'?

Trend 22: Trusted Brands

- Trust is an increasingly critical component of a brand's success.
- Trust takes time to be created, but can be destroyed globally within days.
- The age of a brand is increasingly irrelevant to its level of trust.

Well known businesses with trusted brands have increasing market power in the Digital Age.

After all, if you had the chance to buy from any business in the world, which would you choose?

The Trust Paradox

Trust is now the most valuable thing online. Every business wants to be trusted.

In another paradox of the Digital Age, this thing that is the most valuable online cannot be bought or sold online.

A business cannot force its customers to trust it. Trust has to be freely given to the business by its customers.

Trust can only be earned by the business, and it is usually earned by the progressive keeping of small agreements.

Building trust takes time, but a lot of business online happens very quickly. An already trusted business with an already trusted brand has massive advantages trying to do business in the online world.

In the traditional off-line world, the reputation of a business and the power and value of its brands is important to its success.

In the hyper-congested online world, the magnetic attraction or pulling power value of a trusted brand is magnified enormously, as customers seek the security and safety of proven reputations.

How Can you Build Trust Online?

So, who do you trust online? Who trusts you? More importantly, if trust is so important, how can you actively build it?

UK business consultant, Peter Kneale from Incite puts it like this: *"Focusing too much on trust can become a trap for a brand. Gaining trust is an outcome of doing the right things, not a goal in itself. Trust is not something you can acquire independently of your actions."*

Building trust is an outcome of keeping your promises, but you can also use building trust in your business strategies.

As discussed in Trend 10: Niche Communities, you can develop a strategic approach to establishing your position as a trusted advisor within your target niche communities.

From trusted advisor, you can then work to become a trusted brand leader in your niche.

You can make sure your website has content that builds trust rather than harming it. You can include logos of trusted third parties and authentic real life testimonials and reviews.

On shopping sites, you can provide good guarantee period, show evidence of other customers having been treated well when they claimed on your guarantees and provide free return shipping if your customer are not satisfied.

All these things help, but the best thing to do is to keep your promises and develop a reputation for keeping your promises.

Trust Is Not Based On The Age of A Business

In the off-line world, the age of a business and its brand was a major factor in knowing whether you could trust it or not.

Whilst age still has some importance in levels of trust, very new and young businesses that interact honestly and sincerely with prospective customers and keep their promises are seizing the initiative.

Smart new businesses encourage their happy customers to talk about their experiences online, usually with high leverage promotional exposure through social media and review sites.

Established businesses can't take their ongoing existence and success for granted in the online world, especially if they don't bother with the same high leverage promotional tools used by their smarter and newer competitors.

Trusted Individuals make the Best Trusted Brands

Individuals can become their own trusted brands online. In fact, individuals are often better placed to become trusted brands than are companies.

The provision of helpful advice is often the key catalyst to forming a trusted relationship. Helpful advice generally comes from an individual within a business rather than from a business.

Thus, a helpful and wise individual has more chance of building their reputation and becoming their own trusted brand in the niche.

> ***Helpful and wise individuals can become trusted brands***

You may have strategic opportunities in your business to develop key employees as advisors to your customers and communities. This can promote their reputations for the benefit of your business.

The obvious downside to this is the risk that any employee who becomes the trusted advisor in the niche will leave and either work for a competitor or set up a rival business in competition with you.

It's a real risk, and you obviously need to choose your key employees carefully for this role. There will be a shift in power between you and these employees as their public reputation grows with your customers and within your communities. Think in advance how you will handle this.

If you are the business owner, the smarter approach is for you to take on that role yourself. You become the trusted advisor and you develop that reputation for the benefit of your business without the threat of creating more competitors at your expense.

Managing Your Brand

Brand management online is an emerging area of importance to businesses and individuals.

Managing the online reputation takes skill, care, time, patience and authentic customer-focused sincerity in both actions and reactions.

Within businesses, new roles of Brand Guardians are emerging, with responsibilities to monitor, preserve and enhance the brand in the marketplace.

There are plenty of reputation monitoring tools available online, most of which can search social media networks, blogs, review sites and web pages for mentions of your business and the type of sentiment being expressed about you.

The Growth of the Trusted Brand Monopoly

In another of the many paradoxes of the apparently highly competitive Internet, the growth of a small number of highly trusted online brands brings with it the possibilities of virtual monopolies within certain niches.

Whilst not a monopoly, PayPal has cemented its position as the global market leader in independent payment systems, and so far its rivals have battled unsuccessfully to gain traction against PayPal.

New players find it tough to compete and can be reluctant to enter a market where substantial trust is required and the incumbent market leader already has established trust, good systems and a huge majority of the market share.

For as long as the incumbent maintains the trust and their systems, they tend not to lose market share – even if a new competitor offers a low cost or even free service to compete.

Google Risks Trust With Privacy

Despite its philosophy of"Do no harm", Google has been close to breaching trust in various areas where it collects personal information both online and in the off-line world.

Google has admitted that while taking photographs for its mapping services of the UK, its Street View cars collected emails, passwords and web addresses from wireless networks across the UK.

Google apologized, claiming not to have collected the data intentionally, but it lacked sincerity and damage was done to Google's brand.

Even digital giant Google could be hurt if it gets issues of trust too wrong too often.

Users rely on information they find online, and more so when it comes from a trusted source. As an information provider, you never know how information online will be used or the damage an error may cause.

In November 2010, an error on Google Maps had the border between Nicaragua and Costa Rica incorrectly positioned by 2.7km. The Nicaraguan army moved in, took down the Costa Rica's flag and put up their own flag. It was resolved peacefully this time…

Trust Breaches Will Kill Digital Businesses

Trust is hard to establish but easy to destroy, and you never know which trust-breach straw might break the consumer camel's back

News of trust breaches can virally spread globally within hours or even minutes.

> ***Internet users as a herd could stampede over or away from any business within days.***

The more a user becomes reliant on a service, the harder it is to move away from it. With breaches of trust, Internet users as a herd could stampede over or away from any business on the planet within days.

Retribution from customers and vigilante hackers could be swift and savage. Some trust breaches will kill digital businesses.

Some of the current major global brands like Google and Facebook appear imperialistic, domineering and sometimes almost contemptuous of the masses they attract and serve.

Do we need to remind them that trust must be earned and not blindly given, especially online?

No matter what size the business, building trust today is a key ingredient for achieving business success tomorrow.

Trends Closely Related to Trusted Brands

When you think about Trusted Brands, also think of these trends working in harmony with it:

Trend 3: 24.7 On-Demand
Trend 4: Transaction Speed
Trend 9: Personal Connectivity
Trend 10: Niche Communities
Trend 11: Linked Corporate Ecosystems
Trend 12: Disintermediation
Trend 15: Globalization
Trend 16: 100% Perfect Fit Products
Trend 17: 1 to 1 Marketing
Trend 18: Information Aggregation
Trend 20: Low Cost Software & Cloud Computing
Trend 21: Popular Mass Culture
Trend 23: Peer Recommendations
Trend 25: Consumer Power

Action Principles

As you think about Trusted Brands, think about the 10 Action Principles. What new ideas do these principles give you for the future? What can you do better and smarter?

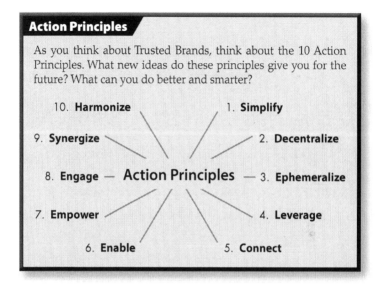

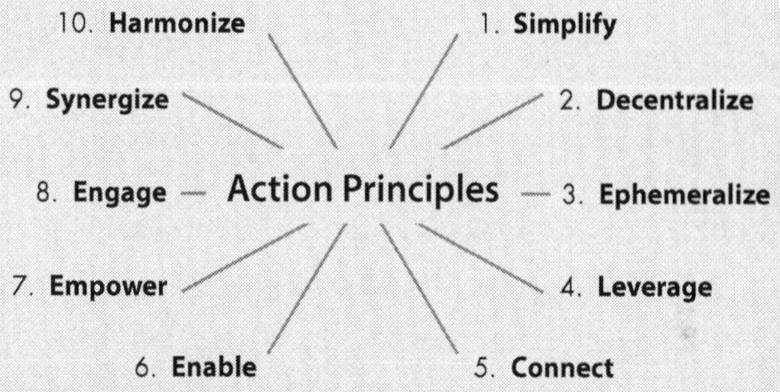

Some Questions To Ponder

1. Who are the most and least trusted businesses in your industry? How have they achieved that trust?
2. Who are your most and least trusted customers? Why?
3. Is your business perceived as a trusted brand? How do you know?
4. How can you improve your levels of trust?
5. What could threaten the levels of trust your customers place in your business?
6. How do you ensure your staff don't jeopardize the trust your customers place in your business? Can you control or mitigate those risks?

Trend 23: Peer Reviews & Recommendations

- Potential customers do pre-purchase research online.
- Honest peer reviews are more credible than any information supplied by the business.
- Positive reviews may help a bit; Negative reviews can hurt a lot.
- Your reviews can help or hurt others.
- Peer reviews rule! Like it, or not.

As the business owner, it may surprise you to learn that your prospective new customers will probably believe the comments strangers make about your business rather than believe what you say about your business.

It's tough, but that's how it is, and it's going to get worse not better until you are trusted in your community and niche market.

People tend to trust the comments and feedback of other customers and their peers much more readily than they do the comments of marketers employed by a business.

You can accept and embrace this, and make it work for you. Or you can ignore it, but ignore it at your peril!

User Generated Content Is Valuable Content

In social media and on many websites, customers are being encouraged to leave comments, reviews and testimonials.

This user-generated content can be very valuable to other people, and on some sites, can be the main value of the site.

As an example, check out the reviews on TripAdvisor.com. These reviews may be incredibly helpful if you are planning to travel anywhere.

A few years ago, my wife and I went to Vietnam. As an experiment, we planned our whole trip around what other people suggested in reviews on TripAdvisor. TripAdvisor reviews helped us select what to see and do, where to stay and even where to eat. It worked for us.

User-generated content is not just about reviews. It is the basis for Wikipedia, the free multi-lingual online encyclopedia, now considered to be one of the most authoritative sources of information in the world due to its user support and its content creation, editing and management systems.

What Is Being Said About You Online?

People may be writing reviews about your business and your products right now.

As the business owner, you need to find out what may be being said about you online. Then you or one of your team needs to respond appropriately.

Far from being negative or damaging, many comments and reviews on review sites are constructive and helpful, even if they are not glowingly positive.

Trip Advisor has a vast range of reviews, and as far as I know, they don't censor, modify or remove reviews. Some are very damning, and these must inevitably affect the business being reviewed.

> ***The smart ones take feedback gracefully and gratefully, and learn from it.***

Even when reviews are negative, this feedback becomes an opportunity to improve, innovate or respond.

How you respond is critical. Some businesses respond aggressively, some defensively and some don't believe a customer could ever have a bad experience with their business.

The smart ones take the feedback gracefully and gratefully, and learn from it. Others ignore customer feedback or pretend to take on board, but nothing changes.

If you are a potential customer of a business, it becomes a great part of your pre-purchase research to learn how a business responds and tries to rectify any bad situations.

If you run the business and get a bad review, you have to assume (and you can almost guarantee) that other people including prospects, customers and competitors will read the review. Some of them will be watching to see if, when and how you choose to respond.

It's amazing that even today, many businesses do not bother to learn what is being said about them, their products and services online, and specifically in sites that may also be visited by other customers and prospects.

Reviews and recommendations are continually being included in comments by users on Twitter and Facebook, and monitoring these can be an important part of a social media and reputation management strategy.

Some niche community sites are becoming industry standard meeting places, and business owners need to know these sites and what is being said about the business.

UrbanSpoon.com is popular in providing reviews of restaurants and cafes around the world, while Yelp.com encourages reviews of shopping, nightlife, entertainment and more.

Google has recently bought the review site Zagat.com which has developed a unique 30 point review rating system. It's likely that Google will be rolling out Zagat-style 30 point ratings for businesses globally.

Word of Mouth has long been the best form of advertising in the traditional off-line world. This hasn't changed online, but the tools and the leverage power have changed.

"An unhappy customer can now tell millions"

Instead of telling one person or telling 50 people, a happy customer or an unhappy customer can now tell millions of people, almost instantly.

Currently, the average Facebook user has 139 friends. A comment made by one person on Facebook can be seen by friends and shared with 'friends of friends' to reach thousands of others in seconds.

Or these comments could sit in a review site for months, waiting for a prospective customer to visit the site, search for your business and read the review.

Once released to the world, these comments may never be able to be questioned, explained, defended or deleted.

It's tough, but it's real. This social proof of how you have performed for others in the past can help you or harm you long into the future.

Trends Closely Related to Peer Reviews

When you think about Peer Reviews, also think of these trends working in harmony with it:

Trend 4: Transaction Speed

Trend 9: Personal Connectivity

Trend 10: Niche Communities

Trend 12: Disintermediation

Trend 16: 100% Perfect Fit Products

Trend 17: 1 to 1 Marketing

Trend 18: Information Aggregation

Trend 21: Popular Mass Culture

Trend 22: Trusted Brands

Trend 25: Consumer Power

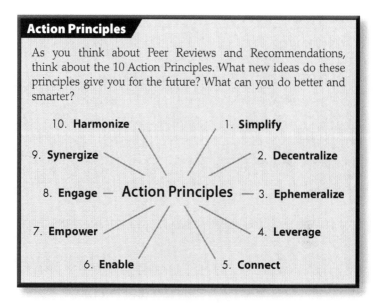

Action Principles

As you think about Peer Reviews and Recommendations, think about the 10 Action Principles. What new ideas do these principles give you for the future? What can you do better and smarter?

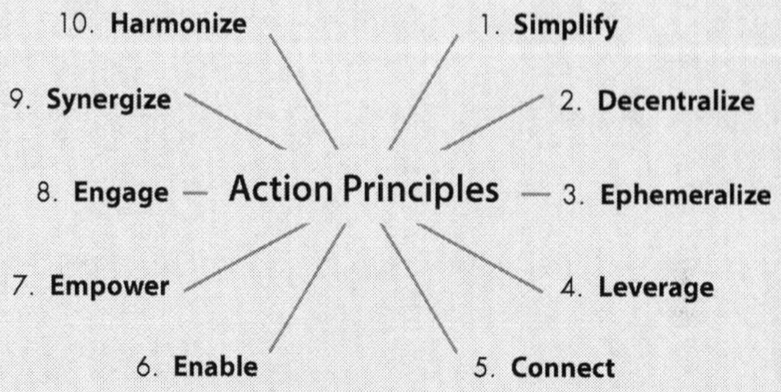

Some Questions To Ponder

1. Do you know where people might be talking about you, your products and your organization? How will you find out?

2. Do you know what is being said about you online? What are you doing about it?

3. Do you encourage and promote your customers to give reviews of your products and services?

Trend 24: Loss of Control of Identity

- The 'Dark Side' is growing as well.
- Hackers are real and hacking is getting easier.
- Your online information is exposed and public forever.
- Don't assume people care about your privacy.

In amongst the many seemingly positive trends the Digital Age is bringing to our businesses and our lives, there is a dark side to the online world.

> ***It's a dark and potentially threatening scenario, but it's real.***

There are new threats and vulnerabilities and our security and privacy is at greater risk than ever before.

We may carefully protect our valuable user names and passwords from someone sitting nearby us, but overlook the threats from viruses and malicious software already living on our computer, device or network.

We may have anti-virus software, but if it is not reliable and up-to-date, then we're at risk.

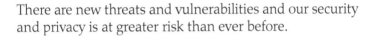

Hacking Tools

We're also at risk from our data being intercepted by others during its transmission through the Internet network. These risks are real and increasing.

On 24 October 2010, a new free program called Firesheep was released as a plug-in for the Firefox web browser.

Firesheep is a hacking tool that allows someone on the same open wireless network as you to view your data packets, read cookies on your computer and access your user name and password to many sites including Facebook.

With this information, a hacker can side-jack your identity by logging in to other websites pretending they are you and adding comments or maliciously attacking you and your information.

The developers of Firesheep claimed they released the software to draw attention to the insecure nature of many websites.

Was Firesheep popular? Within 24 hours the plug-in had been downloaded 8,000 times and within 48 hours it had been downloaded 200,000 times.

By January 2011, it had been downloaded over 1.1 million times and by July 2012, there had been nearly 2.3 million times from the main download site.

Before Firesheep, hacking into open networks required some sophisticated technical skills. This is just one of the tools now easily available. The threats are real and they are growing!

Our Identity

Almost as bad as the threats from hackers are the threats and vulnerabilities we create for ourselves, often without care of even thought about the risks.

We willingly make information about our background and our identity available on social sites, websites and in emails.

We never know who is going to be viewing the information, or when or why.

As transient as an email might be, once sent it is gone forever – but we don't know where it's gone or where it is going to end up.

Emails can be forwarded on easily and quickly to others, sometimes by accident and sometimes very intentionally.

> ***We never know who could view our information, or when or why.***

Information on social sites like Facebook is there forever, and open to abuse in so many ways.

It's not just your personal information such as birthdays, addresses or photos that should concern you.

It's your personal discussions, comments and thoughts often entered quickly on your'wall'or someone else's wall.

Worse, if you use Facebook's email, Hotmail or Google's Gmail, other people including government agencies have the power to access your messages.

We give away our identity and our personal information too easily and too readily, sometimes without thinking about what we're doing.

We blindly assume businesses have good privacy policies, but how often do we read them?

It's a dark and potentially threatening scenario, but it's real, and you may not even know it is happening or who is doing what creepy thing with your information.

Facebook Scans Your Status Updates

Facebook receives plenty of criticism for its abuses of personal information, but it does monitor what is going on.

As reported by Reuters and Mashable in July 2012, Facebook and other social platforms are now watching users' chats for real or potential criminal activity and notifying police if suspicious behavior is detected.

Alex Fitzpatrick of Mashable.com recently wrote, "The screening process begins with scanning software that monitors chats for words or phrases that signal something might be amiss, such as an exchange of personal information or vulgar language.

"The software pays more attention to chats between users who don't already have a well-established connection on the site and whose profile data indicate something may be wrong, such as a wide age gap. The scanning program is also "smart" — it's taught to keep an eye out for certain phrases found in the previously obtained chat records from criminals including sexual predators.

"If the scanning software flags a suspicious chat exchange, it notifies Facebook security employees, who can then determine if police should be notified."

According to Facebook's current terms on its site, it works with law enforcement *"where appropriate and to the extent required by law to ensure the safety of the people who use Facebook...*

"We may also share information when we have a good faith belief it is necessary to prevent fraud or other illegal activity, to prevent imminent bodily harm, or to protect ourselves and you from people violating our Statement of Rights and Responsibilities. This may include sharing information with other companies, lawyers, courts or other government entities."

Tor Anonymity Network

The Tor system is an anonymity network to conceal a user's location or Internet usage from surveillance or traffic analysis.

Users can freely download the Tor software which then allows the user's data to route their internet traffic in an encrypted format through a global network of servers run by volunteers.

Tor has recently been used by dissident movements in Iran and Egypt to protect users' identities and internet usage.

According to Wikipedia, Tor has been endorsed by civil liberty groups as a method to be used by whistleblowers communicating with journalists.

There is a dark side to the Digital Age. Criminals are getting smarter.

Tor has also been used hacker groups and online black markets run by criminal enterprises.

Some of these online black markets such as Silk Road use deeply buried private websites, communication via the Tor infrastructure and the Bitcoin system for exchanging payments.

'Bitcoin is a decentralized electronic cash system that uses peer-to-peer networking, digital signatures and cryptographic proof so as to enable users to conduct irreversible transactions without relying on trust.' (Source: Wikipedia.)

There is a dark side to the Internet and the Digital Age. Criminals are getting smarter, and we have to get smarter too.

Fundamental Shifts?

Many younger users do not seem to be conscious or care about the risks and threats to their personal information, or how it may be used against them now or later in life.

Some observers see this as a fundamental shift in how these users value their personal information. Or is it a lack of care based on the ignorance and naiveté of overly-trusting people living in the connected world they already take for granted.

These Digital Natives have grown up enjoying deep online relationships, access to instant information and an expectation of instant gratification.

For many of them, any problems that may arise later in their life seem a long way off from the enjoyment of today.

Trends Closely Related to Identity Control

When you think about Identity Control, also think of these trends working in harmony with it:

Trend 6: Smart Mobile Devices

Trend 8: Technical Connectivity

Trend 9: Personal Connectivity

Trend 11: Linked Corporate Ecosystems

Trend 17: 1 to 1 Marketing

Trend 18: Information Aggregation

Trend 19: Physical Location

Trend 20: Low Cost Software & Cloud Computing

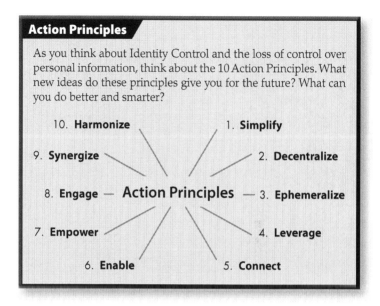

Action Principles

As you think about Identity Control and the loss of control over personal information, think about the 10 Action Principles. What new ideas do these principles give you for the future? What can you do better and smarter?

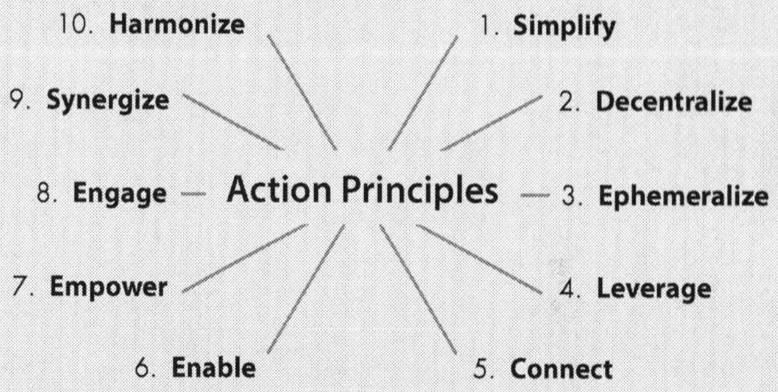

Some Questions To Ponder

1. Is your virus protection software up to date?
2. Do you connect to the Internet through open and insecure shared wireless networks? (e.g. in a coffee shop)
3. If you use Facebook or other social media, have you checked your privacy settings recently?
4. How much personal information do you, your friends and family reveal online?
5. Are you a little bit more concerned about the 'dark side' of the Internet from reading this? If so, what are you going to do about it?

Trend 25: Power to Consumers

- Consumers have the 'Power of Influence'.
- No longer "Buyer Beware." Now "Seller Beware."
- "If you screw your customers, your customers can fight back and publish and organize."

We're long past the days when the voice of the consumer could be silenced online.

These days the consumers' voices should not be ignored either, although some businesses still think they can.

The Internet has empowered consumers with new tools and methods to use their voices and to make sure they get heard.

It's no longer "Buyer Beware." Now it's "Seller Beware."

An upset consumer may not initially be heard by the business that caused the upset, but they will definitely be heard by other people, and sooner or later, by prospective and existing customers.

Eventually, the business will hear and will listen. How the business responds is the key question.

Dave's Bike

A few years ago, a tech-savvy friend of mine (let's call him Dave) had a problem with an expensive new bicycle he had purchased from a bike store.

Dave approached the store, wanting the bike to be repaired under warranty but the bike store denied the claim.

Thinking this was unfair, Dave took his issue online, voicing his complaint in various cyclist forums and discussion groups.

Dave also set up a small website with the domain name being the name of the bike store and then the word disaster.com.

He used this website to outline his situation and describe how the bike store treated him. In a short time, the website "bikestorenamedisaster.com became very well known in Dave's cycling community.

After a while, the bike store contacted Dave threatening legal action for defamation if Dave allowed the website to stay online.

At the same time, the store also offered to repair the bike under the warranty as had been originally requested by Dave.

Dave took the website down and his bike was repaired. Dave achieved his outcome, but the bike store's reputation suffered in the online cycling community and off-line as well.

Dave the tech-savvy consumer had fought back, and won.

Service Levels at Dell Computers

I work on a Dell notebook computer, and have done for years. These days, I generally find Dell good to deal with, but a few years ago, I remember thinking their service levels were pretty poor.

I didn't do anything about their service levels at the time, but another disgruntled customer called Jeff Jarvis did.

Here's an extract from a genuine blog post Jeff wrote about Dell Computers in June 2005 and posted online on his blog.

> *Is anybody at Dell listening? I know you are. What do you have to say, Dell?*
>
> *While you're at it, Dell, go here and here and here and read the comments and see how y our customers hate you. (And that extra space in "your" is because of your broken keyboard, by the way.)*
>
> *A snarker in the comments says, "Buyer beware."*
> *No, we are in the new era of "Seller beware."*
>
> *Now when you screw your customers, your customers can fight back and publish and organize.*
>
> *I just sent this link to Dell's media relations department and told them to read the comments and see what their real public relations look like.*

I'm not sure exactly how Dell Computers responded to Jeff then, but I do know that Dell's customer service levels improved dramatically afterwards.

Jeff was right, and I think Dell realized it and learned from it.

> ***If you screw your customers, your customers can fight back and publish and organize.***

In the online connected Digital Age, it's no longer 'Buyer Beware'. It's 'Seller Beware'.

Consumers have increasing power in the Digital Age. With social media available to everyone online, anyone can give feedback about businesses to the world.

Tech-savvy consumers have a few more tools they can use, and they do use them.

Trends Closely Related to Consumer Power

When you think about Consumer Power, also think of these trends working in harmony with it:

Trend 6: Smart Mobile Devices

Trend 9: Personal Connectivity

Trend 10: Niche Communities

Trend 11: Linked Corporate Ecosystems

Trend 12: Disintermediation

Trend 15: Globalization

Trend 17: 1 to 1 Marketing

Trend 21: Popular Mass Culture

Trend 22: Trusted Brands

Trend 23: Peer Recommendations

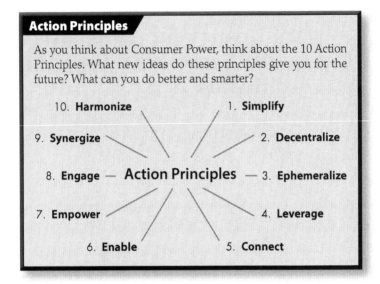

Action Principles

As you think about Consumer Power, think about the 10 Action Principles. What new ideas do these principles give you for the future? What can you do better and smarter?

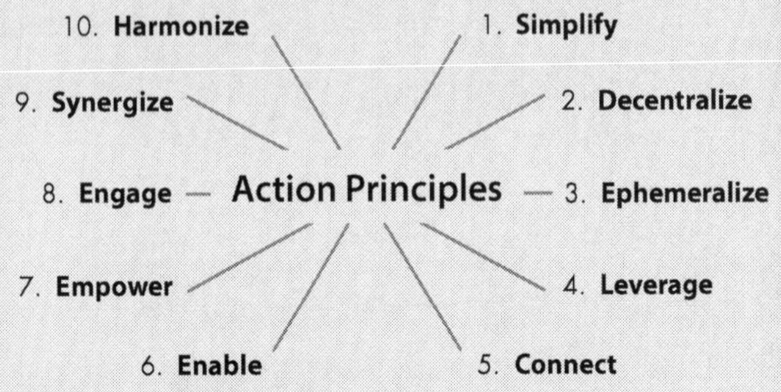

Some Questions To Ponder

1. Do you know how your past and current customers are influencing others?

2. When was the last time one of your customers got upset with your business? How did they react? Who else learnt of it? How do you know?

3. How do your staff members react when a customer gets upset? How do you know?

4. How will you react next time a customer gets upset?

5. How will you make sure there is a positive outcome from the upset?

Your Digital RoadMap

Alice came to a fork in the road.

"Which road do I take?" she asked.

"Where do you want to go?" responded the Cheshire Cat.

"I don't know," Alice answered.

"Then," said the Cat, "it doesn't matter. If you don't know where you are going, any road will get you there."

Lewis Carroll, Alice in Wonderland

To know and not to do is to not yet know

Zen Philosophy

Knowledge might be power,
but only when you take action

What Are Your Options For The Future?

OK, so we've explored 10 Action Principles and 25 Big Picture Digital Age Trends. (Really, we've just scratched the surface, but it's a start.)

What about your business? What are your best options for the future?

Thinking about each Trend has probably raised even more questions for you. That's what this Big Picture planning process is all about.

Asking new and better questions can help you discover new and better answers; and usually different answers make sense for different businesses. Planning your best Digital RoadMap means planning what makes the most sense for you.

If your business is well-resourced, highly profitable and on a positive growth path today, then you may want to skip this chapter and fast-forward to You and Your Pathways on page 199.

BUT

If you are wondering whether your business even has a future in the digital world, this chapter is for you.

What are your options?

Planning your future in the digital age can be a complex puzzle, especially if you are struggling at the moment. There is no single answer to the puzzle, but one thing's for sure… staying confused in the blur is not going to help.

If it feels like you and your business are in a hole, the first thing to do is to stop digging. Stop making it worse.

Maybe you feel like a tiny startled rabbit caught in the headlights of global forces outside your control. The rabbit has to decide to move so it doesn't get run over or shot.

Maybe it feels like you are on a business treadmill, continually running every day, but not getting anywhere.

When you're on the business treadmill, your energy gets drained, stress levels go up, and your effectiveness and results go down. You don't even take time out to think about business planning. You are just too busy during the day and too tired during the night.

Getting off that treadmill can seem so hard, especially while it's going fast. Even the thought of jumping off the moving treadmill is stressful. You just know there will be pain. So you stay on, and keep running. Sound familiar?

In Lewis Carroll's "Through the Looking Glass", the Red Queen said to Alice *"It takes all the running you can do, to keep you in the same place. If you want to get somewhere else you must run at least twice as fast as that."*

Do you have to run faster just to stay in the same place? Is it time to work smarter, not just harder? Is it time to help your hard-working staff work smarter too? Is it time to get off the treadmill? It's your choice!

If you decide it is time to get smarter, there is no point in dabbling with half-hearted or ad-hoc efforts.

It's amazing how many businesses dabble in the online world without really know what they are doing or why.

The Yellow Pages advertising company Sensis conducts an annual e-business survey of Small to Medium Enterprises (SMEs) in Australia.

The 2011 survey revealed that while 95 per cent of Australian SMEs report they have Internet access, and 67 per cent say they have a website, less than 16 per cent reported they have some form of strategy for the digital activities of their businesses.

Surveys from different organizations show a variety of statistics about website adoption and usage, but one thing is for sure. Many websites aren't used strategically and many websites are ineffective.

Many businesses still view their website as simply an advertising tool or as an online brochure.

There's little point running advertising for a business that is struggling or dying unless you also treat the causes of the business problems.

From my experience, the causes are seldom just a 'lack of sales', but more often a lack of effectively implemented business strategies including differentiation to give uniqueness in the market. Usually there is a lack of customer focus, customer service and customer care as well.

Simply having an online brochure won't make customers love you or want to buy from you, especially if they have far better customer experiences dealing with one of your smarter competitors.

Just having a website without having sound digital business strategies may not help you much. It could be a waste of your time, resources and money. Even worse, it could be a waste of opportunities.

Without digital business strategies that make sense for the future, many businesses today will become targets in the smarter digital plans of their smarter and more strategic digital competitors.

These days, business owners need a smart digital roadmap for the future to avoid becoming digital roadkill.

If 84% of SMEs in Australia don't have digital business strategies, and if this figure is roughly similar throughout the Western world, then a lot of businesses are under threat.

The threats are real. Virtually every industry is changing. Sectors such as retail are changing dramatically.

The retail sector is going to be decimated over the next 5 to 10 years. It will probably be far worse than 'decimated'. 'Decimated' means 'one in ten' will die. Ten per cent of traditional retailers seem to be in the process of dying right now.

Which businesses will survive and which businesses will die?

Business owners who don't want to change are obviously at risk; businesses that take their customers for granted are at risk; and businesses that don't understand the digital age and don't plan how to operate in the digital age are at risk.

Of course some old businesses will die. That happens all the time, and as we know, new businesses start using smarter business models and methods.

The low business start-up costs and low barriers to entry offered by online technology will see new competitors emerge to service markets, communities and niches locally and globally.

The most successful new businesses are likely to be those that build agility into their core business. The ability to quickly Plan, Do, Learn, Improve, Grow and Do Better will be critical. Some entrepreneurs describe it as the ability to Fail Fast and Fail Forward.

Here you are, operating your business in this environment... and maybe trying hard not to fail. **What are your options?**

Option 1: Business As Usual

You could simply keep doing business the way you've always done it and see what happens.

Right now, someone somewhere may be scheming how to steal your best customers from you or how to headhunt your best staff.

'Business As Usual' is a risky approach, and very risky for an already struggling business.

Option 2: Stop The Bleeding and Act Smarter

Some businesses are in lots of trouble at the moment, losing money and using up their reserves to stay alive in the hope things will get better.

We're in the middle of massive structural change. The digital world is causing a lot of it, and it's not going away. Things won't get better unless you make them get better.

If your business is bleeding money today, you need to do what it takes to stop the bleeding.

This always calls for tough decisions. Unfortunately, many businesses in trouble decide to reduce their advertising and marketing, stop spending on staff training, and cut staff employment numbers and costs.

As the business owner, you probably want to do whatever it takes to save your business and keep it going, but you also know you have to be careful not to destroy your business strengths and capabilities in the process of cutting costs.

Your tough decisions involve making smarter plans to help you and your remaining team see a clearer and brighter future.

If you make smarter plans, then make a digital roadmap to show your planned pathway, give you clarity in the blur and give you the vision for your brighter future.

Option 3: Stop The Bleeding And Stop The Business

If you really are bleeding and you can't see a bright future at all, then stopping your business now could be a smart option.

There is no shame in ceasing to operate your business if that is the best decision. It's usually worse to make no decisions at all, especially if you also make no smarter plans for the future.

It's hard to take but quick pain may be better than long pain. You and your team may feel a lot more pain for a longer time if you allow your business to endure a slow and lingering death. (I'm not trying to be brutal, but ongoing agony and stress is miserable. Life is way too short to spend years of it being miserable.)

Option 4: Plan Your Exit

Is it time to exit your business? Is it time to cash-in now and better use your resources and experience when you move on to something else?

Almost every business owner looks for exit strategies sooner or later. Selling your business now or soon could be smart, and you may want to prepare for it.

Preparing a business for sale, selling it and exiting gracefully typically takes one to three years. (I've been involved in seven different business startups and exits over the years, with many learning experiences and varying results.)

If you plan to sell your business, you'll probably get a better price if you can show your business is prospering in the digital age rather than being a victim of it.

Developing your own digital roadmap may be more than just a useful exercise for you. Your roadmap will be valuable to help you focus your activities wisely as you prepare for the business sale.

Even more importantly for you, a smart digital roadmap for your business could make your business substantially more valuable so you get more money when you sell the business. The acquiring business may pay more for your business if they think the strategies and actions in your smart roadmap could be better used in their own business plans.

If your business and brands are seen to grow as leaders in your marketplace in the digital world, the acquiring business is likely to value the goodwill factor of your business more highly.

If you can show your business has substantial growth potential, the 'blue-sky' associated with your business valuation is likely to increase.

If you want to sell your business in the next few years, then start planning now how to get potential acquirers to value you more highly so they may pay more to acquire your products, brands, systems, loyal customers and smart employees.

Option 5: Make Non-Digital Your Strength

If you really don't want to run a business in the digital world, then you may find a non-digital business niche in your marketplace.

You could stay local, stay off-line and seek to attract those customers who value the 'old-fashioned' approach of great customer service and strong local relationships.

It's a bit like the 'Slow Food' movement in Italy, where traditional old-style cooking and very long lunches set the Slow Food movement restaurants apart from other faster food newcomers in the marketplace.

There will probably be businesses all over the world making 'old-style traditional' business practices into one of their points of market differentiation.

Perhaps non-digital business methods could be turned into strengths for your business. Keep reading this book so you know what you'll be going up against.

Option 6: Catch Digital And Act Smarter

If you know you need to change and you've decided it's not time to exit or quit, then it is time to act smarter.

Think smarter, plan smarter and then act smarter. Get up to speed with the digital age. Catch the digital waves rather than ignoring or fighting them. See the opportunities that will make sense for your business future. Make opportunities your focus. Find your pathway in the digital world.

You and Your Pathway

Your digital pathway will be unique for your business, and you can choose to take small steps or big steps in your journey.

In my experience, an ongoing series of small well-planned steps is often easier, especially as you move from the known into the unknown.

Most people will not want to go into a scary unknown future, so each of the steps you take also needs to create bridges for your customers and staff to move along with you.

Embrace your customers. Think about what your customers want today and may want tomorrow, not just what you think they needed or wanted yesterday.

Think how you could make your products and services more convenient, more valuable, more available and more effective for your customers.

Embrace your staff. Ask your staff how your business can be smarter and better help your customers. Your staff will know things about your customers and your business that you don't know.

Embrace the online world and embrace smarter digital strategies. Embracing digital business strategies does not mean just focusing on technology.

Technology changes too quickly – and at best, technology only provides tools for you and others to use for some purpose.

There are thousands (or maybe millions) of different digital age tools available to you. Focusing on the technology tools gets confusing if you don't have sound business strategies for using the tools.

> ***Strategy starts with purpose. Why does your business exist?***

Strategy starts with purpose. So, what is your purpose? Why does your business exist? What do your customers want from you? What opportunities do you help your customers enjoy? What are the customer problems your business tries to solve?

How could you make things more convenient for your customers? How could you empower your customers to do more with less and get better results? How you could be doing business tomorrow?

Creating Your Digital RoadMap

Here's a digital business planning framework you may want to use to create your Digital RoadMap.

This is not trying to create or re-create the entire business plan for your business. Your Digital RoadMap is a summary of your planned pathway in the digital world.

Your RoadMap becomes part of your business plan, but we're not trying to create yet another business plan that sits around gathering dust.

Many business plans are huge big documents that take a lot of time to prepare, no one really owns and often no one bothers to read them anyway. You probably don't want or need that

From my experience, what is more helpful is a simple overview clearly showing your planned pathway forward.

It's important this overview is well thought out and:

- ☑ Clearly shows where your business is headed;
- ☑ Clearly shows the strategies you plan to use;
- ☑ Has clearly defined stages and goals for your actions;
- ☑ Is easy to understand, share and explain to others; &
- ☑ Will inspire your team and keep them on track.

Think of your Digital Roadmap as a two page, high level overview that will help take you from (A) where your business is today to (B) where you want your business to be at some point in time in the future.

Where you are today is pretty easy to define, but the future point in time may be a little harder. What is the planning horizon that makes sense for you?

Some businesses may have the capacity to work on 20 to 50 year planning horizons, but from my experience, most don't.

A 3Year horizon is often a good point to start. Of course, you might want to look further ahead - 5, 10 or even 20 years. Perhaps you can see your future in 10 years time but perhaps you can't. Every business and every industry is different.

For some business owners, seeing the Big Picture of the business in even 3 years time is a stretch, but 3 years can usually work for most.

I recommend keeping your RoadMap to two pages. Remember the Action Principles and Simplify.

Planning your 2 page RoadMap encourages you – and sometimes forces you – to keep the RoadMap at a high level Big Picture view. Of course, you can link this two page high level view to more detailed action plans as you go along, but start with the Big Picture view.

Let's repeat that. Start with the Big Picture view for your industry and business. Think how your business may operate in the future and where you can best fit in to your industry and niche.

Develop the high level strategies that make sense for you to catch the digital waves and create your future. After that you can start developing your action plans, and selecting the tools and technology you might use.

If you let the technology tools drive your business, then you may find yourself constantly confused about what technology you should be using – and why. You'll make ad-hoc, short-term decisions and stay in the Blur, rather than enjoying better results from your Digital RoadMap.

From my experience, that's where many people go wrong. They go straight to thinking about their action plans and focus on the technology and the tools rather than their business vision and strategies.

As an example, many people jump into building their new websites, getting a new mobile app developed or using some new social media tool without really thinking about the purpose and long-term strategies of their business. They avoid these strategic questions, and go straight into action.

Making it up as you go along is fine as long as you know where you are going.

Typically, this type of action-first person tells me they are really busy. So I ask them, "Are you busy going in circles or are you busy going in straight lines?" It's usually circles.

The other important reason for keeping your Digital RoadMap to two pages is that it is easy to view the pages and share them with your team if you can summarize your digital business future and your pathways onto two pages.

You could produce a 50+ page document, but let's face it, probably no one will read it. If you ever print it out, it will just sit on a shelf and grow old and out-dated like most other business plan documents.

Better to simplify it. Create it so you can print it out and stick it up on your wall by your desk, by the water cooler or the coffee machine. Make sure you share it.

You need it to inspire yourself and others on your team. Save it for viewing on your digital device as an image, PDF, screensaver, wallpaper or whatever.

The key is to make it visible. If it just lives inside your computer as yet another document, it'll be invisible. You know the old saying, "Out of sight is out of mind". That's very true in today's world of clutter, noise and too much information.

You need to share it so you and others can focus on it, live it, believe it, make it happen and succeed with it.

Paul J Meyer, Founder of the Success Motivation Institute says "Success is the progressive realization of your own pre-determined worthwhile goals".

That's what you are doing here with your RoadMap. Setting and then progressively realizing your business goals, and doing it with smarter digital business strategies.

You are setting yourself up for success.

Let's look at the outcome you want from this first creation of your Digital RoadMap.

Digital RoadMap Framework Sheet 1: Big Picture & Digital Strategies

The result you want from the planning process is to produce a clear summary of your Big Picture view and key Digital Strategies on one page.

Use the strategies to outline how your business will operate to make that Big Picture future view a reality.

You may like to use mind maps and other graphical ways such as info-graphics to present this information clearly on one page so it is easy to view and understand. Or you may prefer to use a table format with bullet points.

On the following page there is a sample mind map. I like this mind map format, but frankly, the format doesn't really matter.

Provide enough detail to make the strategy clear, meaningful and unambiguous.

List your chosen strategies and group them in ways that make sense for you and your business.

As a guide, developing strategies in the following areas or groups could be helpful to you:

- Business
- Products
- Customers
- Communities
- Marketing
- Sales
- Website
- Mobile
- Ecosystem
- Technology
- HR-People

There is a more detailed list in Step 2 of the 10 Step planning process.

> Business planning is a team game.
> Who is on your team?

Digital RoadMap Framework Sheet 1
Big Picture & Digital Strategies

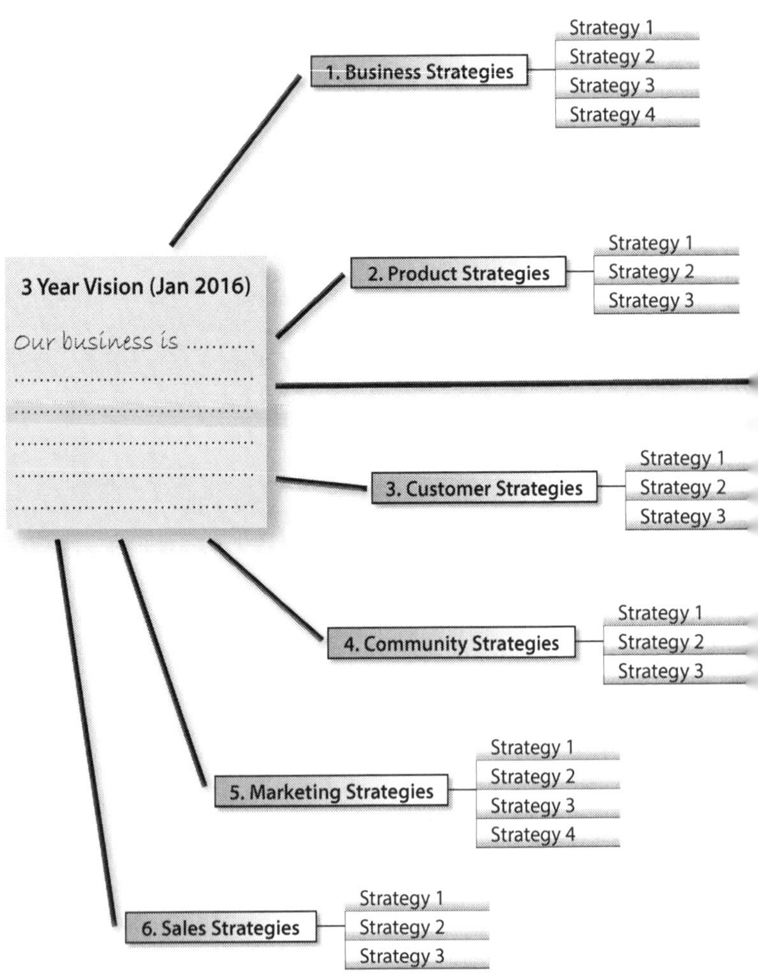

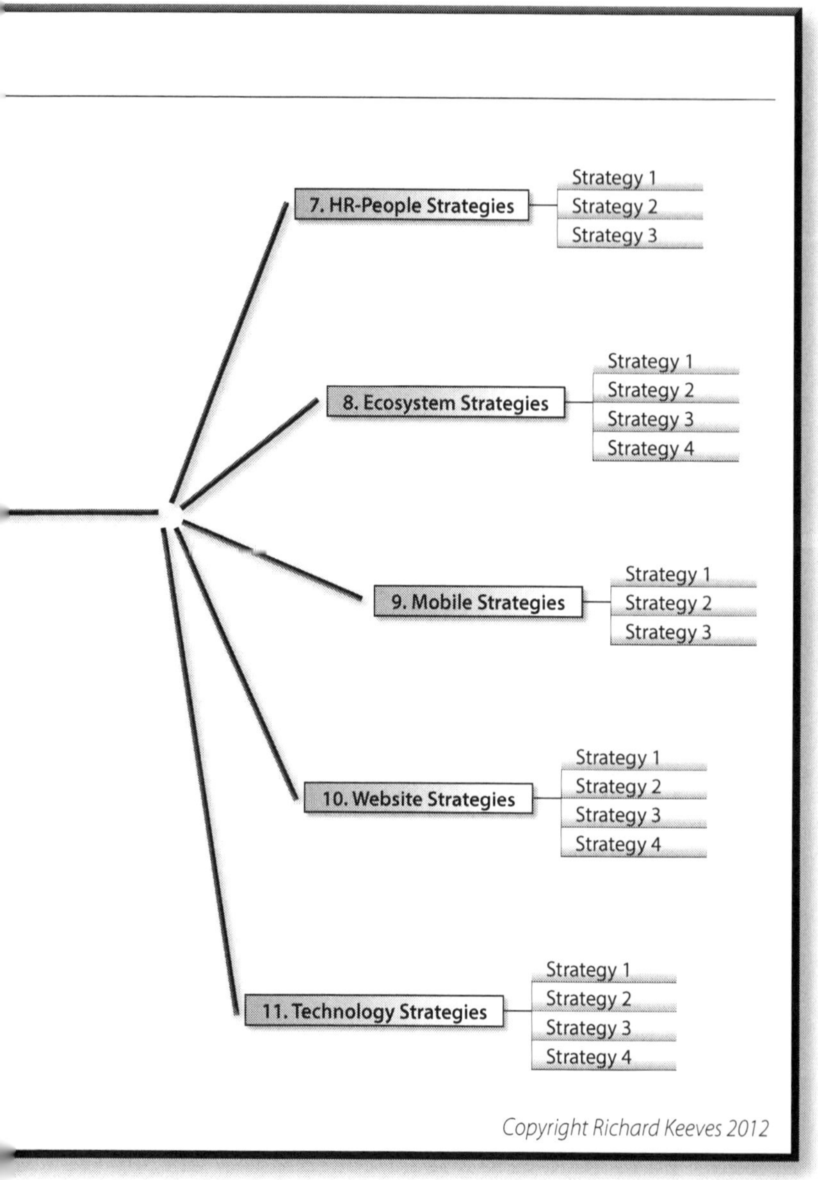
7. HR-People Strategies
Strategy 1
Strategy 2
Strategy 3
8. Ecosystem Strategies
Strategy 1
Strategy 2
Strategy 3
Strategy 4
9. Mobile Strategies
Strategy 1
Strategy 2
Strategy 3
10. Website Strategies
Strategy 1
Strategy 2
Strategy 3
Strategy 4
11. Technology Strategies
Strategy 1
Strategy 2
Strategy 3
Strategy 4
Copyright Richard Keeves 2012

Digital RoadMap Framework Sheet 2: Stages & Goals

When your Big Picture vision and strategies are clarified, you and your planning team can work on your roadmap to get where you want to go.

Using the Stages and Goals framework layout, summarize your roadmap onto one page to show the most likely stages of the most likely best pathway to implement your strategies. This makes it easier to focus on, understand and clearly explain to others in your business. You will also probably want to share your roadmap with digital service providers and IT partners you engage to help make it happen.

It doesn't have to be perfect. You are planning where you want your business to be in 3 years time. Your pathway will be less clear the further you look into the future, but it will become clearer as you work along the journey. Accept that. Don't stress on it, and don't use it as an excuse for inaction now.

Understand where you are today, and then focus on where you want to be in 3 Years time. Work backwards to where you want to be in 12 months time, and think what you can do in the next 12 months to get there. When you break the next 12 months into smaller bite-size 3 month segments, it will become less daunting and more achievable.

At the minimum, plan your stages and goals for the next 3 years, the next 12 months and the next 3 months. If you can, look at what you want to achieve over the next 12 months and split this into 3 month blocks with stages, milestone outcomes and the goals you can achieve each 3 month period.

You may be familiar with the need for SMART goals: Specific, Measurable, Attainable, Realistic & Timely. You may also want to have Minimum, Realistic and Stretch targets for some or all of these stages and outcomes.

Sheet 2 becomes your 'current' best plan of your pathway. It's your guide for the future and yes, you will need more detailed action plans with action to make it a reality.

Your Digital RoadMap will be fluid. Your business will change, and your customers' wants and expectations will continually evolve, perhaps more quickly than you can currently imagine.

New technology will emerge to allow new things to be done, or done sooner than you had planned. Your customers will use the new technology and new services you and others provide, and this adoption will happen at different times for different customers. Your RoadMap needs to continually evolve.

It's smart to review and update your Digital RoadMap regularly. If you update it every 3 months and roll it forward as you progress along your pathway, you will always have your roadmap looking 3 years ahead with smaller 3 month blocks clearly defining the path for your business.

Digital RoadMap Framework Sheet 2
Stages & Goals

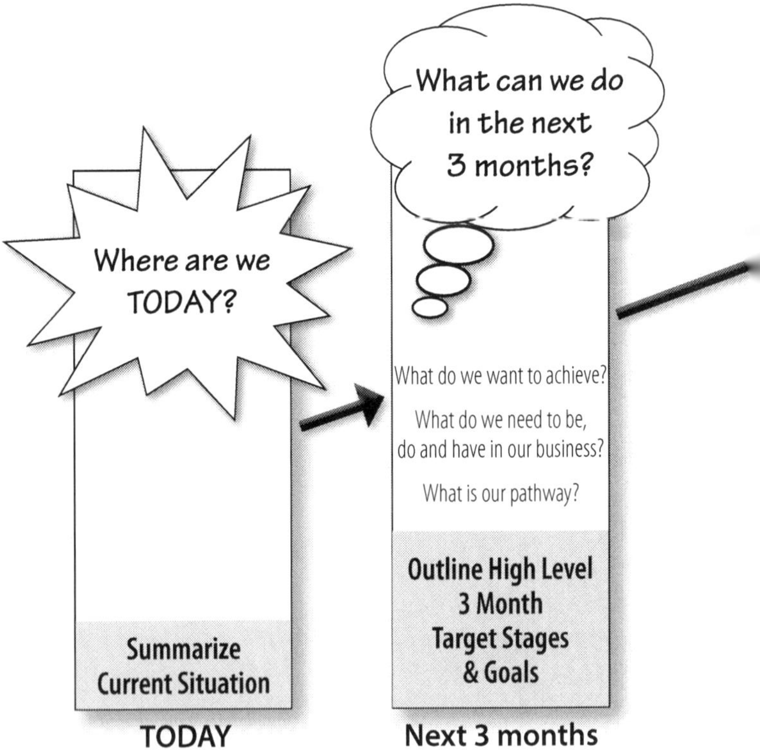

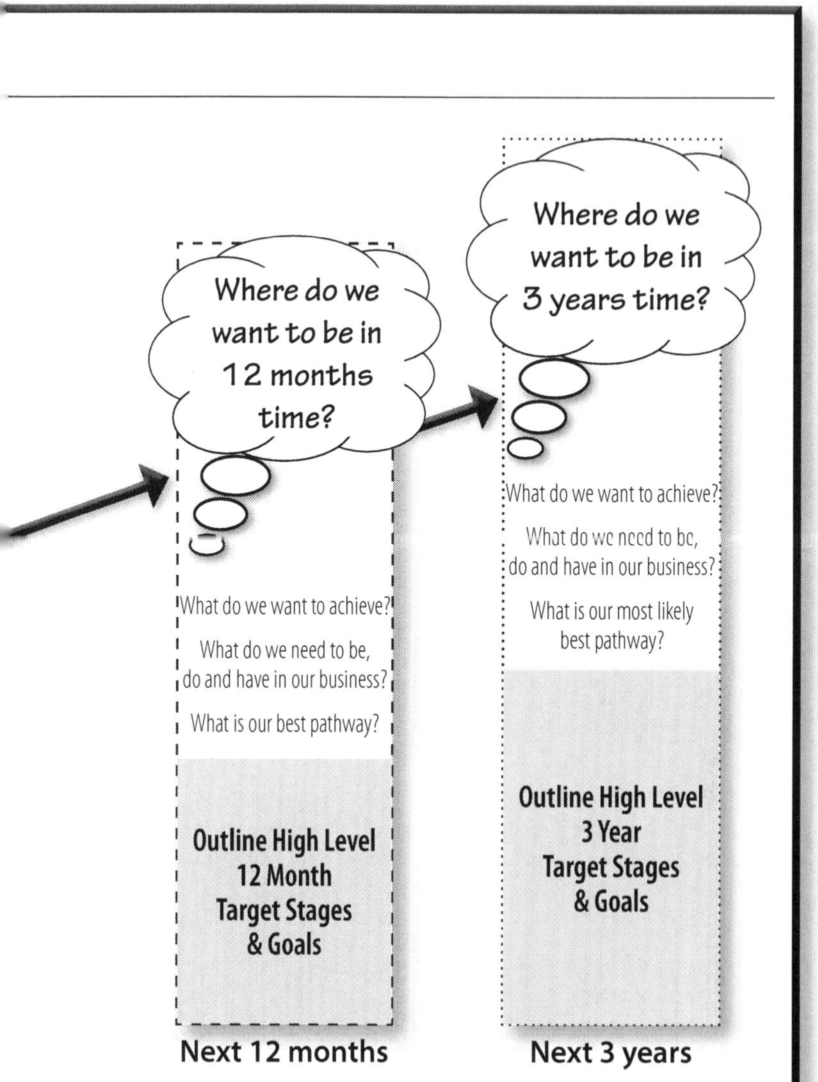

Where do we want to be in 12 months time?
What do we want to achieve?
What do we need to be, do and have in our business?
What is our best pathway?
Outline High Level 12 Month Target Stages & Goals
Next 12 months
Where do we want to be in 3 years time?
What do we want to achieve?
What do we need to be, do and have in our business?
What is our most likely best pathway?
Outline High Level 3 Year Target Stages & Goals
Next 3 years

Quick Summary

Sheet 1 outlines where you are going in the future (Big Picture view) and how you intend to achieve this future (Strategies).

Sheet 2 outlines your current view of the most likely steps along your pathway (Stages and Goals).

That's your Digital RoadMap.

Of course, there is a lot more to be done to plan and implement the Digital RoadMap, but with your RoadMap to guide you, you and your team will know where you are going and why.

You'll need to define the details of tasks within each 3 month block. In addition to Sheets 1 and 2, you'll need to create your Action Plans for each stage. Define the detailed tactics, tasks, actions, capabilities and resources you'll need.

Choosing the best tools, technology and helpers to assist you is usually a challenge. You can't do it all yourself so you'll need appropriate helpers to work with; internal people, external providers, partners, suppliers, contractors and advisors. Make smart decisions for your RoadMap… and make sure you stay flexible for the future.

Now let's work through some questions to help develop your Digital RoadMap in the 10 Step Planning Process.

10 Step Digital RoadMap Planning Process

To start with, here's an overview of the planning process.

STEP 1: Review Your Business, Value & Web Presence

Ask Three Starter Questions

Q1. What do you want to achieve? (Purpose, Objectives)
Q2. What customer benefits & value do you provide?
Q3. What could you be doing better online?
What is Your Unique Selling Advantage? (Your USA)

How can you build Convenience, Trust, Value & Pay-Off?

STEP 2: Develop Your On-Trend Vision & Strategies

What are the likely implications & impacts of the 10 Action Principles and 25 Digital Age Trends on your

Working with the Principles and Trends,

a. What is the likely future for your industry & business?
b. What strategies make sense for your business?
c. How can you become The Chosen One?

How can you build Convenience, Trust, Value & Pay-Off?

STEP 3: Explore Your 5 Ps

What could you do to

- Improve Your Productivity?
- Improve Your Practices
- Improve Your People
- Improve Your Products?
- Improve Your Processes? (ICEPT)

How can you build Convenience, Trust, Value & Pay-Off?

STEP 4: Study Your Benchmarks

Find comparisons & learn from the sites, processes, products & service levels of

- Your industry leaders
- Remote local & global competitors
- Business leaders

How can you build Convenience, Trust, Value & Pay-Off?

STEP 5: Re-Discover Your Key Customers

Re-discover what customers want and value

- Current & future likes, dislikes, suggestions
- Look beyond the obvious. Don't assume.
- Develop Key Profiles & Typical Personas of your ideal customers and how you help them.

How can you build Convenience, Trust, Value & Pay-Off?

STEP 6: Learn To Lead Your Community

How can you lead your Community?

- Connect, join in, belong and contribute.
- Understand their common purposes & different values.
- Learn more of their pains, wants, needs & desires.
- Add value without expecting instant reward.
- Become a Trusted Advisor.

How can you build Convenience, Trust, Value & Pay-Off?

STEP 7: Grow & Connect Your Ecosystem Network

Strengthen your links with your Supply Chains and Sales Channels.

Find new alliances, Joint Ventures, collaborators inside and outside of your current communities and networks.

- Complementary & Co-operative businesses; Alliance businesses & people
- Add value to your customers for Mutual benefit

How can you build Convenience, Trust, Value & Pay-Off?

STEP 8: Learn From Your Competitors

Study your Evolving Competitors

- What are they doing better than you?
- How will you stay ahead?

Become Your Revolutionary Competitor

- What could make your business obsolete?
- How would you put a business like yours out of business? can you make

How can you build Convenience, Trust, Value & Pay-Off?

STEP 9: Find Technology Gaps and Opportunities

Customer Focus (External)

- What will help your customers? What will they expect?

Business Focus (Internal)

- What do you need for your business?

Technology-Driven Focus

- What improvements can come from technology?

Gap Analysis

- What do you have? What do you need? What are the gaps?

Open, Pre-built, Secure, Reliable, Integratable,
Easy to implement & learn, Low cost, High ROI,
High Flexibility, Low Risk, Good options for the future

How can you build Convenience, Trust, Value & Pay-Off?

STEP 10: Decide Your RoadMap

- Review Opportunities & Strategies
- Assess business cases for options
- Assess capabilities & resources
- Focus on Convenience, Trust, Value & Pay-Off
- Develop Big Picture view (3+ Years)
- Decide best strategies (1 year & 3+ Years)
- Plan RoadMap Stages & Goals (3M, 12M, 3Y)

Plan in 3 Month chunks

Step 1: Your Business, Value & Web Presence

The Three Starter Questions

To start with, consider three main questions...
Question 1: What do you want to achieve?
Question 2: What benefits & value do you provide?
Question 3: What could you be doing better online?

Question 1: What do you want to achieve?

- ❑ What is your business purpose?
- ❑ Why does your business exist?
- ❑ What are your business objectives?
- ❑ What makes you different in the marketplace?
- ❑ What do you need to be able to do really well to grow and prosper?

Question 2: What benefits & value do you provide?

- ❑ What are the benefits and value your customers receive now from you and your products and services?
- ❑ What benefits or value are they likely to want or expect in the future?
- ❑ How do you build relationships and trust with your customers?
- ❑ What value factors are important to your customers?
- ❑ Why do they choose you?

Question 3: What could you be doing better online?

- ❑ How is your business using online systems to give your customers benefits and value now?
- ❑ How can you make better use of online systems in the future?

Planning Questions

- ❑ What value does your website provide your customers?
- ❑ What are your customers' Reasons To Visit? (RTV)
- ❑ What are their Reasons To Return? (RTR)
- ❑ How is your website working for you? How do you know?
- ❑ Look at your client information, communication, education and trading systems. How effective are they? How do you know?
- ❑ Consider your use of online systems now. What is working well now?
- ❑ How is online helping your customers? How is it helping you? How can you improve it further?
- ❑ What is not working well now? How is it harming your customers? How is it harming you? How can you improve it? What do you need to get right?
- ❑ For the future possibilities, ask how will an online service help your customers?
- ❑ When will your customers expect you to be able to provide it?
- ❑ How will it help you? When could you do it?
- ❑ Are the technology tools available today? If not, what is their horizon?

- ❑ What will you need to get right?
- ❑ How can you build on your points of difference?

How can you create more
Customer Convenience,
Trust, Value and Payoff?

What Is Your Unique Selling Advantage?

We talk a lot about differentiation and the need to be unique. Why? Because consumers have never had so many choices.

You need to break through the clutter so they know the WIIFM (What's In It For Me?) benefit if they choose to deal with you.

What makes your business different to your competitors? What makes you stand out in the marketplace?

You could call this your 'Unique Selling Proposition' or USP. I find the 'Unique Selling Advantage' (USA) concept from marketing expert Michael Ross an easier approach.

Here are two ways to discover your Unique Selling Advantage.

Discovery Method 1: List the five unique reasons I should buy from you. Focus on the benefits for your customers.

For some businesses, this approach can be difficult. Having 'great service' is not a USA. Great service these days is simply an entry level requirement, but one that many businesses still don't achieve.

If you don't know what these five reasons are, pick up the phone and call some customers, or ask them when they come in. Tell them you're doing some research. Ask them to tell you the reason they chose your business. You may discover something your customers know that you haven't thought about. Whatever it is, promote it!

Discovery Method 2: Create two lists. One is called "You know..." The second is called "What we do..." Then you compare your business to other businesses.

In the first list you write the key problems customers typically experience when dealing with your competitors and your industry.

If you don't know, have you ever 'Mystery shopped' them? Send a few friends to shop at your competitors' businesses, and get them to fill out a feedback form and return it to you. You'll get valuable feedback as to what these competitors are doing, what they're doing well and what they're doing poorly.

In the second list, you write what your business provides, making your advantage the opposite of the bad points of your competition.

Then you turn these into sentences and paragraphs.

"You know how when you buy from others you often get…"

"What we do is…"

To make sure you highlight the benefits for your customers rather than just the features of your product or service, add "so what this means to you is..." to your sentences and paragraphs.

You can self-critique your work by asking yourself "So what does this mean for customers?" or just "So what?" when you read each sentence.

Drill down into your answers by continually asking "So what?" This is one way to look deeper than 'the obvious' and find the benefits behind the benefits.

These 'benefits behind the benefits' may not be those you immediately associate with your products or services.

They could be more basic human needs or desires such as being accepted, admired, appreciated, free, important, in control, loved, respected, safe, trusted, useful, valued or worthy.

Make your benefits strong and deep. Focus on what makes your business unique. Marketing specialist Barry Urquhart says, "It is better to be different than it is to be better". He's right, but being different AND better is best.

Your USA is not permanent. It must evolve as your customers and your business evolve. Review your USA frequently; reviewing it as part of your 3 Monthly Digital RoadMap planning process can be very valuable.

There's an example of my own current business USA on the final page of this book. It evolves...

Step 2: Develop Your On-Trend Vision & Strategies

Step 1 was about reviewing your business as it is today.

How about the future? If you work with the 10 Action principles and catch some of 25 Digital Trends, what could be the future for your industry and your type of business? How could your business operate'On-Trend'?

Unless you work with a 50 year planning horizon, you don't need to look 50 years into the future. Try to look 10 years ahead, then bring it back to 5 years ahead, and then, assuming you're working on 3 Year Digital RoadMap, focus on 3 years ahead.

What could your industry and your type of business look like in 3 years' time? Where will you fit in? Where do you want to be? Where could you be?

Use the Action Principles and Trends for inspiration.

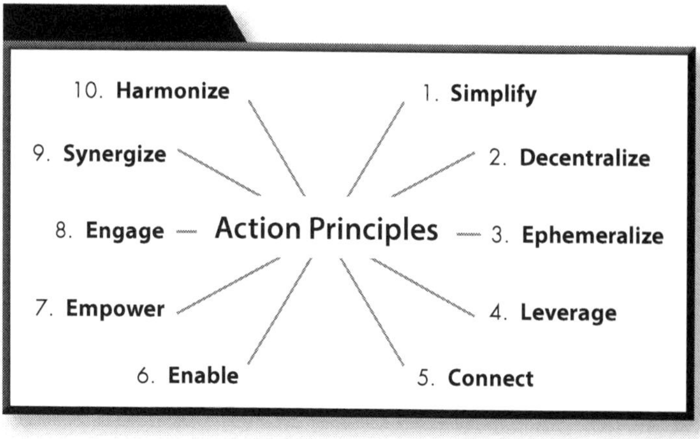

If you apply the Action Principles to your industry, what could be your future for your business? What strategy ideas can you learn or develop from them?

Look back through each of the trends and think about how they have already impacted on your customers, your products, your business and your industry.

Think about the trends that seem most relevant to your industry. Look at combinations of trends and how they could impact on your customers.

Developing Your Vision & Strategies

Your 3 Year Horizon
Look ahead. Picture your business in 3 Years time.

How could your business be operating? How could your business be structured? How could it evolve? What can you see for your business on your 3 Year horizon?

Take a look through these key areas as you think about your future vision and possible strategies. This is not intended to be a comprehensive list but rather this can be a starting point. Some may not apply to you; perhaps many could…

A. Your Business

1. Unique Selling Advantage evolution
2. Smarter & more sustainable Business Models
3. New and smarter Revenue and Profit Streams
4. Cost Reductions through smarter purchasing
5. Expense reductions through smarter operations

6. New Capital Raising for smarter growth
7. Partnerships based on new synergies
8. Better planned Exit Strategies

B. Your Customers

9. Tighter focus on your Preferred Niches
10. Better definition and attraction of Ideal Customers
11. Better service to Customers at their Locations
12. Smarter Customer Relationship Management
13. Improve Customer Experience
14. Improve Customer Communications
15. Better use of Customer Reviews
16. Smarter Sales Strategies
17. Better Fulfillment systems
18. Smarter and better use of Customer Databases
19. Better Customer Research
20. Improve levels of Trust
21. Focus on Customer Convenience
22. Investments in Customer Convenience
23. Define and improve Value to customers

C. Your Products

24. Improve effectiveness of Distribution Channels
25. Turn Disintermediation to your advantage
26. Create and sell 100% Perfect Fit Products
27. Improve Products through planned Internal Leapfrog
28. Smarter Digital Enablement of Products
29. Use Convergence to improve offerings

D. Your Communities

30. Find, create or lead powerful Community Networks
31. Add sustainable Value to chosen communities
32. Build Trust within chosen communities
33. Become the Trusted Advisor in chosen communities

E. Your Marketing

34. Smarter & more effective One to One Marketing
35. More accountable Advertising
36. More use of better Lists
37. Smarter use of smarter Databases
38. Harnessing the power of Social Media
39. Getting Found more easily online
40. Better Search Engine Optimization (SEO)
41. More focused Catchment Areas
42. Mobile Marketing for mobile customers
43. Proximity Marketing to attract nearby customers
44. More effective Local Marketing
45. Responsive Reputation Management

F. Your Sales

46. More effective Sales Channels
47. Enhance Shopping Processes
48. More appropriate Information Provision to customers
49. More Customer-friendly Transactions
50. Smarter use of Video
51. Rapid and accurate sales Fulfillment
52. Better and faster Trackable Delivery systems
53. Better understanding of different needs of Local and Global customers

G. Your People

54. Attracting the best or the right Human Resources
55. Better management of Contractors
56. Improve Productivity
57. Matching your expanded Capabilities requirements
58. More effective Training Needs Analysis
59. Better training processes
60. 24.7 On Demand Training (Right Time, Just In Time)
61. Out-Sourcing to improve capabilities
62. Off-shoring to reduce costs
63. Off-shoring to attract talent on large scale
64. Building Local or Global "Best Teams"
65. Improving your 'People Management' Processes
66. Smarter Work Practices for your People

H. Your Ecosystem

67. Smarter Linking of Supply Chains
68. More effective and efficient Sales channels
69. Finding New Collaborators
70. Forming New or improved Alliances
71. Mutually Profitable Joint Ventures
72. Adding synergy with harmony to your Networks
73. Smarter Integration of your systems with others
74. Maintaining Flexibility for the Future

I. Your Mobile World

75. Development of specific-purpose mobile Apps for Key Customers
76. Improving customer experience based on you knowing or tracking each customer's Location

77. Attracting and servicing customers in your Proximity
78. Mobile Information Delivery, 24.7 On Demand or Just In Time.

J. Your Website

79. More effective eStore systems
80. Smarter comparisons to competitors and Benchmarks
81. Better Self management of web systems
82. Smarter Use of Open Source if/when appropriate
83. Always improving System Flexibility
84. Adding capabilities for Systems Integration
85. Integrated Customer Relationship Management systems
86. Improved Web Partner selection, capabilities, management, and flexibility
87. Better presentation of Products
88. Improve online Merchandising
89. Smarter Technology Systems
90. Faster Transaction processing
91. Taking Secure Payments 24.7
92. Better use of Video
93. Planned and trackable Customer Pathways
94. Smarter Tracking and analysis
95. Improve monitoring and use of Website Feedback

K. Your Technology

96. Smarter Software Selection
97. Better Choice of Technology Partners
98. Improve Technology Support

99. Consider Open Source vs Proprietary systems
100. Consider Cloud Platforms vs Self Hosted systems
101. Regular Reliable Backups
102. Improved Security
103. Added System Flexibility
104. Smarter Systems Integration capabilities
105. CRM integration
106. Tech Partner Flexibility

L. Your Competitors

107. Improve Benchmarking
108. Deeper Research
109. Predicting and recognizing Disruptors

Become The Chosen One

It may almost seem too simple, but to be more successful in the online digital world, one of the key areas to focus on is how to be chosen more by your customers.

How can you and your business become the preferred choice in your marketplace?

- ☑ **Be Chosen More By More Existing Customers**
  What can you do so your business is chosen more frequently by more of your existing customers?

- ☑ **Be Chosen More By More New Customers**
  What can you do to be chosen more by new customers?

Here are some online strategic objectives to consider.

Strengthen Customer Relationships

1. Strengthen and protect existing customer relationships.
2. Become the preferred supplier in your local area.

Help Educate Customers

3. Educate your customers and prospective customers.

Build Trust & Credibility

4. Become the most trusted supplier in your industry or business category.

Build Your Valuable Customer Database

5. Build your customer database and use it to drive profitable repeat sales.
6. Build your database into an incredibly valuable and highly saleable asset of your business.

Increase Customer Service levels

7. Make your business & brand world-famous for outstanding customer service.
8. Make every moment of truth with your customers very positive for them.

Increase Customer Convenience

9. Make it simple, fast and easy for your customers to do business with you.
10. Make it easy for mobile customers to do business with you.

Encourage Positive Word of Mouth

11. Become remarkable and encourage your customers to recommend you to others.

Increase Prominence

12. Make sure your prospective customers can find you more easily.

Build Your Eco-System

13. Build and reinforce alliances and collaborative relationships to enhance your marketing, sales, offerings, brand and market position.

Build Better Pathways

14. Build better online customer pathways to your business and your points of sale.

Planning Questions

- ❑ Which trends have already impacted on your customers?
- ❑ Which are likely to impact in the future?
- ❑ What does this mean for your strategic options?
- ❑ Which trends are most likely to influence how you can change your business or your products to deliver more benefits and greater value to your customers?
- ❑ What can you change to be on-trend and operate better, faster and/or at a lower cost?
- ❑ How can you work with these trends to give your customers more of what they value and want, and to better solve more of their problems?

How can you create more Customer Convenience, Trust, Value and Payoff?

Step 3: Explore Your 5 Ps

How could you improve your

1. Productivity?
2. Practices?
3. People?
4. Products?
5. Processes?

1. Improving Your Productivity, Practices & People

As you know, productivity is a measure of efficiency. How efficient is your business? How much output can you produce with specific inputs or in a specific time?

How well skilled and well trained are your people? How well equipped with tools and systems are they? Is your team great today? What are you doing to make your team even greater for tomorrow?

How do your various work practices help your business grow in the online digital world? Do you think some of your work practices might be limiting or restricting your growth for the future?

If flexibility is one of the keys to success in tomorrow's world, then could today's work practices, regulations and laws designed to protect your people and your industry today actually make them more vulnerable tomorrow?

How do you keep your business growing and doing more with less without placing additional unrealistic expectations on an already stretched business?

How do you change entrenched work practices that may constrain your growth and competitiveness?

Parkinson's Law

Back in 1955, Cyril Northcote Parkinson wrote what was intended to be a humorous essay for The Economist magazine. The first line of the essay was *"Work expands so as to fill the time available for its completion."*

Although based on the work practices of the British Civil Service, many businesses around the world could relate to it and the sentence became internationally known as Parkinson's Law.

It entered mainstream business thinking as both an amusing truism and an important lesson to bear in mind when trying to increase productive efficiencies.

From my experience, Parkinson's Law still holds in many organizations. This is not to say that people intentionally stretch work out for as long as they can, but without boundaries and timeframes work times often do expand. If the timeframes are too tight, then people may be forced to take short-cuts to meet deadlines.

How do you decide how long a task or process should take? How can you get more done in less time?

In this faster Digital Age, how do you use smarter systems, technology, tools, processes and practices to get things done better and faster?

Within your business, who allocates records, tracks and reviews the time for tasks? What tools do you use? How good are they?

How can you improve productivity, practices and your people in the future? How can your business better use digital world processes, services, tools and technologies? Even more importantly, how can you plan for these improvements in your Digital RoadMap?

Asking these types of questions is part of the process of moving forward; the answers will vary for different businesses, industry sectors, countries, cultures and regions.

In the past, the answers would have varied depending on the size of the business itself and the resources it has available but now complex and sophisticated improvement solutions are becoming readily accessible at a low cost even for small businesses.

Here are some tools and ideas for improvement you could consider implementing now or later in your Digital RoadMap.

- ❑ Replace your staff email communication with an enterprise social network such as Yammer.com. Yammer is like Facebook but designed for use within an enterprise. It can be a user-friendly way of communicating and recording conversations and information rather than email. Microsoft has just bought Yammer so it probably has a bright future.
- ❑ Set up a Wiki knowledgebase to record the corporate intelligence within your business.
- ❑ Use an enterprise-wide document access, storage and retrieval system to quickly find documents in your office computer networks.

- ❑ Use instant messaging platforms, but be careful of the increased interruption factor they can introduce.
- ❑ Use Voice Over Internet Protocol (VoIP) phone systems and videoconferencing rather than insisting on face to face meetings.
- ❑ Encourage more remote off-site telework.
- ❑ Use more efficient CRM systems to track customer activities.
- ❑ Use enterprise resource planning systems to better plan and track who is doing what when.
- ❑ Automate escalation procedures in the event that a task is overdue or late.
- ❑ Use remote web/Cloud based project management systems for task allocation. (Check out Asana.com which is free for workgroups of up to 30 people,)
- ❑ Think about out-sourcing your local networking and IT support to a reliable Cloud-based provider.
- ❑ Automate your data backups by using Cloud-based back up services.
- ❑ Allow your staff to each have multiple computer display screens on their desks so they can have multiple windows and workspaces open at once.
- ❑ Only allow staff to interrupt each other with trivia at certain times or never.
- ❑ Turn off incoming email alerts. Check your email when you want to, rather than when an email comes in. (In the 4 Hour Work Week, Tim Ferris talks about using email auto-responders to wean your colleagues and even customers off email. Rather than perpetuating instant responses to email, you change the expectations of others about when you will check, read and respond to emails.)

- ❑ Use file-sharing tools like Dropbox.com to synchronize the sharing of files between staff and customers.
- ❑ Use web tools like MindMeister.com or FlockDraw.com to express and share ideas visually with people in different locations.
- ❑ Add frequently requested information to your website or intranet. FAQs have been around for a long time online – because they work as a way of addressing problems, educating customers and prospects and reducing support costs.
- ❑ Create instructional videos for your customers and add them to YouTube or Vimeo to explain how your products work.
- ❑ Use 'Read Later' tools like Instapaper.com to save web articles you come across while you are working so you can read them when you're not trying to work.
- ❑ Use tools like Evernote.com to collect, store and track information.
- ❑ Use webinar tools such as GoToWebinar.com, ClickMeeting.com or AnyMeeting.com to provide training and webinars to customers, prospects and staff.
- ❑ Use social media management tools like Hootsuite to easily access and update your different social media networks.
- ❑ Use online training providers to get your staff up-skilled. Check out Grovo.com and Lynda.com for globally available training courses.

- ❑ Use computer screen-recording tools like RescueTime.com to monitor what you do and where you could be wasting your time. RescueTime also allows you to be in 'focus mode' and block out induced web interruptions.
- ❑ You may use Microsoft Outlook or some other calendar and task management system. Task management tools like TaDaList.com may be helpful for keeping your 'To Do' lists under control. Getting Things Done (GTD) is a popular personal workflow management system for knowledge workers.
- ❑ Think about expanding your team with people located elsewhere in the world. Check out services like oDesk.com, Freelancer.com and eLance.com
- ❑ Can your business create one of the Best Teams in your niche? (Refer Trend 15 Globalization for details.)
- ❑ If you don't have your own Personal Assistant or secretary, get yourself a full time or part-time Virtual Assistant located somewhere in the world. You can find them locally or perhaps put a job posting on a site such as oDesk.com.

This is just scratching the surface of improvement tools online. You can find more at SmarterWebStrategies.com.

How can you create
Customer Convenience,
Trust, Value and Payoff?

2. Improving Your Products

You provide products to your customers, generally to satisfy a known want or need, but sometimes customers don't know they want a product until it is provided for them.

Visionary new product and services can change the product landscape in industries and create whole new categories. Apple's iPhone and iPad devices are two contemporary examples of new categories of products.

As Daniel Burrus says, this type of visionary product *"gives the customer the ability to do what they can't do, but would have wanted to do, if they only knew they could have done it".*

What matters most is not the product itself, but the benefits the product provides to the customer when they own, use or consume the product.

Take another look at Trend 14: Mass Customization. Could your products be individually customized for different customers and yet produced on a mass scale?

Review Trend 16: 100% Perfect Fit Products. Can you develop products that are 100% right for a niche group of your customers?

Planning Questions

- ❑ How can you use online technology to improve your products?
- ❑ What are the strengths and weaknesses in your current products?

- ❑ What research have you done lately? What assumptions are you making?
- ❑ When was the last time you made major improvements to your products?
- ❑ What simple changes could be made easily that would add substantial value to the product?
- ❑ How can you include online components in your off-line products?
- ❑ What digital products could you have?
- ❑ How can you mass-customize some of your products?
- ❑ How could you develop 100% Perfect Fit Products?

How can you create Customer Convenience, Trust, Value and Payoff?

3. Improving Your Processes

Online processes could perhaps be included in many areas of your business, but which online processes will make the most sense to you and your customers?

When should you be introducing new or improved online processes in your Digital Roadmap?

You may recall the ICEPT Transaction model discussed with Trend 4 (Transactions).

In the ICEPT model, transactions are either
I Information Transactions;
C Communication Transactions;
E Education Transactions;
P Production Transactions;
T Trading Transactions; or
Various combinations of these.

Processes surround every transaction the business makes. It may appear obvious but it's important to remember that processes have inputs and outputs. Outputs in one part of a process are often inputs for a secondary or later part of the process, or for a totally separate process.

> ***Your customers won't want badly disconnected processes***

The ability to integrate and connect the outputs and inputs of different processes becomes increasingly important when you want to improve processes.

Processes that can't be connected and integrated become fragmented. Fragmented processes are often slow, cumbersome, prone to errors and expensive, and neither you nor your customers will want badly disconnected processes in an otherwise well-connected world.

Processes need to be consistent and predictable. The process itself should pick up errors and ideally be self-correcting.

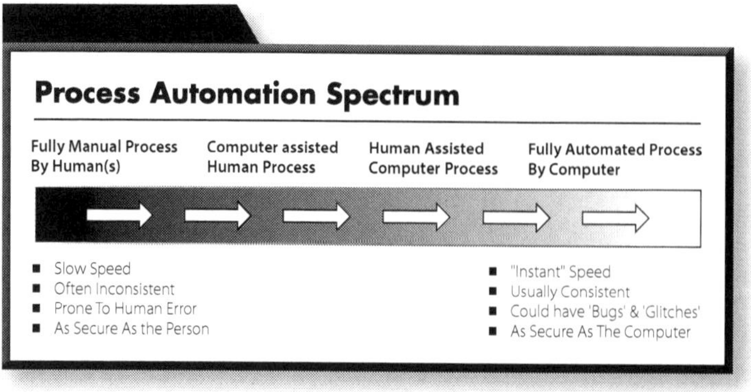

Many organizations have processes that are undefined, unstated, not documented, and often left to the person running the process to follow unwritten guidelines.

If you try to speed up or automate undefined, bad or disconnected processes, the result is usually chaos.

Automating Your Processes

Digital Age tools can be used to improve and automate processes and their outcomes. The abundance of possible online tools makes this both potentially rewarding and potentially risky.

Many organizations already use hybrid processes with computer-assisted manual processes or human-assisted automation.

Every process in your business today could be placed somewhere on the spectrum. Sooner or later, most processes move along the spectrum, generally towards becoming more automated.

Workflow modeling tools can assist in helping to improve your processes. It can be an important area for making big improvements and it is worth getting expert help and guidance.

> ***What business processes can you make more automated?***

Planning Questions

- ❑ What customer processes are you using online already?
- ❑ How are they working for you? How are they working for the customer?
- ❑ Which of your customer processes can move or need to move on the spectrum, and when? How?
- ❑ How accurate is your customer database? How do you currently use it?

How can you create more Customer Convenience, Trust, Value and Payoff?

Step 4: Study Your Benchmarks

Find comparisons & learn from the sites, processes, products & service levels of

- Your industry leaders
- Remote local & global competitors
- Business leaders

Whatever the nature of your business, there will be other websites and online systems you can use for comparisons to learn ideas and options that may be working for them – and may work for you.

If you operate locally, find other similar local businesses to yours but who are operating in a different geographic region or country and not competing with you. Make contact with them, and see what you can share and learn from others.

Also, look for the businesses in your industry that are considered the leaders. Look at global competitors in your field.

Look for other leaders in your type of business – retail, wholesale, manufacturing, etc. Look to see who is doing what well, and what you can learn.

You can learn from similar businesses to yours, and you can also learn plenty from others who are doing well – even if they are in totally different business areas.

Learn to look behind the obvious 'first impression' stuff of design appearance. Some of the best benchmarking can come from looking at the processes used by leading businesses in other industries.

As an example of processes, what could a hospital learn from website customer care processes used by 5 star hotels?

Learn from the Winners of Web Awards

To help you think outside the box, look at the winners of reputable web awards. Just winning an award doesn't always tell the full story about a website, but it can be a useful place to start to see who is doing what well and getting recognized for it.

Here are nine web award websites you might find helpful to include in your benchmarking toolbox. Some web awards are able to be bought, but as far as I know, the award programs listed here are independent and credible. What can you learn for your business?

1. Web Marketing Association's WebAward
   www.webaward.org
2. Webby Awards
   www.webbyawards.com
3. Interactive Media Awards
   www.interactivemediaawards.com
4. The Australian Web Awards
   www.webawards.com.au
5. The Awwwards
   www.awwwards.com/winners-list

6. New Media Awards
   www.newmediaawards.org
7. The American Advertising Federation"Addy Awards"
   dvserver.net/addy2012
8. CLIO Awards
   www.clioawards.com
9. The Andy Awards
   www.andyawards.com

In your benchmarking, learn to look beyond the obvious. Look for the strategies, not just the obvious tactics and tools being used.

Planning Questions

- ❑ How do your benchmark businesses operate online?
- ❑ What are they doing better then you?
- ❑ What are you doing better than them?
- ❑ What new things have they just released?
- ❑ What new things could they working on?
- ❑ What trends are they working with?
- ❑ How do they add value?
- ❑ How do they build trust?
- ❑ What can you learn from them?
- ❑ What can you copy from them?
- ❑ What can you improve on?

How can you create more Customer Convenience, Trust, Value and Payoff?

Step 5: Re-Discover Your Key Customers

- Re-discover what your customers want and value
- Current & future likes, dislikes, suggestions
- Look beyond the obvious. Don't assume.
- Develop Key Profiles & Typical Personas of your ideal customers and how you help them.

Talk with some of your key customers and research them in more detail to find out what they like and don't like about your current offerings, services, website and customer-facing online systems.

Try to uncover the underlying reasons why they think and feel as they do and ask for their suggestions how you could improve.

Encourage them to share any ideas they have about the future of their industry, and how a business like yours that services them may operate in the future to meet their future needs and wants.

Focus on the value and the benefits for the customer. Remember, at this stage, all ideas are welcome. Look beyond the obvious. Ask them about some of the ideas and options you've identified so far.

Ask them what they think, and how much value some of the new services you are thinking about for the future could have for them.

Develop a profile of your customers, especially the type of key customer that you would like to be appealing to and attracting to your business.

Develop a picture persona and profile for your ideal customer. Make it personal.

Your Ideal Customer is real. With the abundance of the online world, if you can define them you can find them.

More importantly, if you make exactly what your Ideal Customer wants, they can and will find you.

Make abundance work for you.

> ***"Develop profiles and personas of your Ideal Customers"***

<u>Planning Questions</u>

- ❑ Who are your customers?
- ❑ What do your customers value from you?
- ❑ What do they like and dislike about your current products, services and online systems?
- ❑ What are their key issues?

- ❑ What is important to them or could become important? (Improved transaction speed, ease, security, efficiency, cost, convenience, customer service, availability, support, etc, etc)
- ❑ How could you help your customers to help their customers?
- ❑ What do they want from you online?
- ❑ What do they like about your website?
- ❑ What do they think are their Reasons To Visit? (RTV)
- ❑ What do they think are their Reasons To Return? (RTR)
- ❑ Where do they go? What do they do? What do they like? What do they dislike?
- ❑ What do they suggest for improvements?
- ❑ What are their thoughts on "the Future"?
- ❑ What do they want, need or expect from you now? How about in the future?
- ❑ Who else could be your customers?
- ❑ Who are your Ideal Customers?
- ❑ What does your Ideal Customer want from you?

How can you create more Customer Convenience, Trust, Value and Payoff?

Step 6: Learn To Lead Your Community

How can you lead your Community?

- Connect, join in, belong and contribute.
- Understand their common purposes & different values.
- Learn more of their pains, wants, needs & desires.
- Add value without expecting instant reward.
- Become a Trusted Advisor.

Your community or communities exist online and offline, and can include your customers, prospects and potential prospects. Your communities could be local, regional or national, and these days may be global whether you know it or not.

You may service different market niches and be part of different communities. The more you can clearly define the interests of different communities, the more effectively you can cater to them and lead them. Extend your thinking to include anyone interested in your market niche and anyone servicing and supplying that niche. Be careful how you approach researching your communities as your competitors are there as well.

You need to define the common purposes shared by members of your communities and understand the possibly different values of community members.

As social media and community specialist Laurel Papworth says, *"We come together on a topic but divide on how it should be addressed. This creates story, interest and passion. As we enter into the social economy, we learn that those that stand for nothing fall for anything (Alexander Hamilton) and that is not what your consumer wants from you. You had better stand for something. Where is your online community strategy making strong statements? Where is your social media campaign clearly identifying with a community value?"* (LaurelPapworth.com)

You want your community to trust you. Be careful what you say, say what you mean, and mean what you say. Give first before you try to take. Do what you promise. Connect with your community, join in, belong and contribute. Become a Trusted Advisor in your field rather than just another product or service provider. (See Trend 10: Niche Communities.)

Planning Questions

- ❑ What value can you add to the community?
- ❑ How could you add this value?
- ❑ What can you do to build trust?
- ❑ What are members of your community looking for online and not finding?
- ❑ What opportunities are there for you? How can you lead your community?
- ❑ Are you a 'Trusted Advisor'? How can you become one?

How can you create more Customer Convenience, Trust, Value and Payoff?

Step 7: Grow & Connect Your Ecosystem Network

Strengthen your links with your Supply Chains and Sales Channels.

Find new alliances, joint-ventures, collaborators inside and outside of your current communities and networks.

- Complementary & Co-operative businesses
- Alliance businesses & people
- Add value to your customers for Mutual benefit

You probably already work with a variety of other businesses that help your business. Some assist in your sales and distribution channels to help you promote, sell, deliver and support what you do. Some may help you find, source and produce your products and services.

Other businesses may provide you with business-related services to help you operate, while businesses such as banks, finance companies and professional advisors provide access to resources, knowledge and skills when you need them.

These businesses form your corporate ecosystem. The closer and more effectively you can work with your ecosystem to improve and speed up your business, the better you will be able to operate in an increasingly high speed world – as long as you can maintain your agility to grow as you want and your flexibility to cope with change along the way. (See Trend 11 for more on ecosystems.)

Supply Chains and Sales Channels

As highlighted in Trend 12, sales and supply chains and channels are being disrupted by disintermediation. Some middle-men businesses are disappearing and others are being re-defined. New and smarter middle-men are emerging to continually change the landscape.

The value of the middle-men businesses is usually based on what they add to their up-stream suppliers and down-stream customers; and on the strength of their connections and relationships with these suppliers and customers.

If you're a middle-man business, then what is the value you add? How can you add more value and build stronger and more powerful digital world connections? How can you develop stronger relationships with both suppliers and customers? How can you strengthen the links you have and connect more deeply?

Alliances & Collaborators

When you start looking online for people or businesses you can work with to build your business you will probably be amazed at the different opportunities you will come across with others willing to set up mutually beneficial relationships with you.

You may already include some of these people and businesses in your corporate ecosystem. Others you may like to bring into it on a short-term or long-term basis. They may currently be inside or outside of your communities or may be part of different communities that interact with yours.

The opportunities for new synergies are enormous. Some may help you streamline your information, communication, education, production and trading (ICEPT) transactions and processes by helping you to find new or better inputs or new ways to reduce costs or friction.

Other businesses can help you improve your products and services by adding components of their own, or by adding their ideas and information. These businesses may have products you can sell on some basis, or they may be able to help you sell your products.

You may find alliances and collaborators who help you with an ongoing stream of valuable and vital information, advice and benefits you can share with your customers.

Online affiliate sales and marketing programs can provide you with new high leverage sales channels where others can promote your products online in exchange for a sales commission paid to them for new customers they introduce to you. Affiliate sales systems can be fully automated and are relatively easy to establish. It's a smart approach to expanding your ecosystem, especially if you are selling online.

Remember abundance and synergy, and think collaboration and creative cooperation. Part of the key to alliance building is to give value to others first, rather than just looking to see what you can get for yourself. Mutual benefit is the key; the other guy has to win too. The easier you make it for others to win, the faster you will probably win as well.

Planning Questions

- ❑ What online ecosystems do your customers belong to already?
- ❑ What ecosystems could your customers and suppliers join? How could this impact on you?
- ❑ What ecosystems could you join or create to strengthen your business?
- ❑ Do your technology systems allow your alliances and ecosystem network to connect with you?
- ❑ How can your systems be improved so you can integrate more effectively with these other businesses?
- ❑ Who will have most of the power in your ecosystem? If it is not you, how will you protect your business? If it is you, how will you make sure the others are happy and protected in your environment?
- ❑ Make a list of 20 possible new alliances for your business. Go on… start now.
- ❑ What value can you add to each of the alliances? What do you bring to the table?
- ❑ What value could they add to you? How?
- ❑ How will you build trust with each of them, and them with you?

How can you create more Customer Convenience, Trust, Value and Payoff?

Step 8: Learn From Your Competitors

Study your Evolving Competitors

- What are they doing better than you?

Become Your Revolutionary Competitor

- What could make your business obsolete?

Change in the digital age is a combination of rapid evolution and occasional disruptive revolution.

For this digital age business planning process, let's look at three key types of competitor: **Static, Evolving & Revolutionary**.

Your Static Competitors exist in a static comfort zone with a traditional view of your industry. They don't pro-actively change, are slow to react and may even be asleep on the job.

They will wake up and learn to change through survival necessity or they may die in their sleep.

Your Evolving Competitors

Evolving Competitors make strategic or ad-hoc incremental changes to their business to provide more value by offering new or enhanced products and services utilizing new methods and systems.

Evolving Competitors may have a good understanding of digital age trends.

They may have their own Digital RoadMap and make sound decisions to achieve both short-term and long term objectives, or they may just be lucky in their choices.

Consider your Evolving Competitors and how they already have been changing their products or business operations.

Select two or three key Evolving Competitors to start with. Look at what they have done well, and then look at their weaknesses.

Look to see what they have done that you can implement in your own business plan.

Evolving Competitors: Planning Questions

- ❑ Which digital trends appear to be influencing or driving them in their actions and reactions in the marketplace?
- ❑ What trends do they seem to have ignored?
- ❑ What are they doing better than you?
- ❑ How can you catch up and over-take them?
- ❑ What will you need to do to get ahead?
- ❑ What value do they add to their customers? How do they do it?
- ❑ Do you know the Unique Selling Advantages of each of your key customers?

- ❑ What are the reasons for their customers' to visit the websites of each of these key competitors? (RTVs)
- ❑ What are the reasons for these customers to return to each of their websites? (RTRs)
- ❑ How do they build trust?

Your Revolutionary Competitor

Sooner or later however, a Revolutionary Competitor may emerge who partially or totally disrupts your industry.

This Revolutionary Competitor may be new to your industry or may be a green fields off-shoot of one of your existing competitors.

They understand digital age trends and have been focused on finding and providing highly effective digital age solutions that address the same customer problems as you do but deliver more benefits and value faster, better and at a lower cost.

This competitor will not let themselves be hamstrung by their past or current operations.

They may be starting fresh without unprofitable legacy customers, out-dated legacy systems; unwanted legacy staff or expensive legacy suppliers.

They may have no corporate ego or negative baggage. Their previous market reputation may be neither positive nor negative, with no one liking or disliking them. They have no past successes that make them feel complacent or arrogant in the marketplace.

They could have a better product with better benefits, better customer service and deliver it faster, more conveniently and at a lower price than you.

They may have ample funding, can quickly built their new brand, establish a credible reputation and become trusted in the marketplace.

> ***What would happen if your business lost its best customers?***

The Revolutionary Competitor that could hurt you the most would be one whose strategy is to go after your most profitable and juiciest customers and entice them away.

Despite your previously secure position, your business could start to lose its best customers.

For the purposes of this planning process, YOU are going to imagine taking on the role of the Revolutionary Competitor. (Yes, it's a role-play with yourself, but it may not be just 'make-believe' – it could easily happen.)

So here is your question...

If you were the Revolutionary Competitor wanting to put a company like yours out of business, what would you do?

Revolutionary Competitor: Planning Questions

- ❑ Which trends could you work with to make your old business obsolete?
- ❑ If you were free of the legacies of your existing business operation and free of your products, systems and staffing, how would you set up the business differently?
- ❑ How could you operate this business?
- ❑ What could you have on your website? What Reasons to Visit (RTV) and what Reasons To Return (RTR)?
- ❑ What products could you have that will deliver more benefits and greater value better, faster at a lower cost?
- ❑ What could your products look like?
- ❑ How could your products operate?
- ❑ How could you build trust?
- ❑ What are the risks and threats to your current business from a real revolutionary competitor?
- ❑ Which of your current competitors are likely to become Revolutionary Competitors in future? What will you do about it?

How can you create more Customer Convenience, Trust, Value and Payoff?

Step 9: Find Technology Opportunities and Gaps

Customer Focus (External)

- What technology improvements could make real differences for your customers?
- What technology systems, tools and improvements will your customers be expecting and demanding?

Business Focus (Internal)

- What technology improvements do you need now and for the future to achieve your business objectives?

Technology-Driven Focus

- What improvements in technology could make a real difference for your business and your customers?
- What opportunities could new technology systems and tools create for your business now and in future?

Gap Analysis

- What technology do you want or need?
- What technology do you have already?
- What are the gaps?
- How and when can you fill the gaps?

Focus On

- Pre-Built, Open, Secure, Reliable, Integratable, Scalable, Proven
- Easy to implement and learn
- Low or affordable cost & potentially High ROI
- Low Risk
- High Flexibility & Good options for the future

As you have been working through the planning process, you have probably already identified technology opportunities and gaps where you can improve your business with better or smarter technology in the future.

In this planning step, think about your customers, your business and then focus on new technology offerings.

Customer Focus

Customer-Focused improvements are either driven by customers or predominantly for customers.

These are externally focused, looking out from the organization to its customers.

- ❑ What ideas have come to you for using technology to make real improvements for your customers?
- ❑ What technology systems, tools and improvements do you think your customers will want, expect or demand in the future? When are they likely to want these?
- ❑ How can you use better technology to improve your customers' experiences with you?

- ❑ How can you use better technology to make your products and services more convenient for your customers?
- ❑ How can you improve your business processes to make a real difference for your customers?
- ❑ How can you add value to your products and services and make them more valuable for your customers?

Remember, not all customers are the same. To some customers a new feature you add using technology may be seen as a useless gimmick, but to others it may be a major enhancement providing substantial benefits from dealing with you.

Business Focus

Business-Focused Improvements are those coming primarily from your perspective to improve your business.

These come from looking inwards towards your business and your business systems. This focus also includes looking at the systems you use to interact and integrate with your corporate ecosystem.

- ❑ What better technology systems do you need to achieve your business objectives and implement your business strategies?
- ❑ How can you use better technology systems, software and tools to improve your business operations?
- ❑ How can you use better technology to reduce your costs?
- ❑ How can you improve the ways you deal with your suppliers, alliances and others in your ecosystem?

- ❑ How can you use better technology to streamline and improve your processes?
- ❑ How can you use new techno-tools to create better new products and services?

Be careful with this internally-focused approach. Ultimately, everything comes down to how you can better serve your customers.

How can you use better technology to make your products and services better, cheaper, faster and simpler to produce and deliver… while also being better and more convenient for your customers?

Technology-Driven Focus

Many improvements come as a result of new technology providing businesses with new capabilities.

- ❑ What improvements in technology could make a real difference for your business and your customers?
- ❑ How can you use new features in systems you have to add more benefits?
- ❑ Are you fully using the available features in your existing systems? What can you be doing better with what you have already?
- ❑ What opportunities could new technology systems and tools create for your business now and in future?
- ❑ How do you know what is available now and what is coming on the horizon? How can you find out?
- ❑ How could you use synergy to combine different components together to create something new?

Gap Analysis

Part of your planning needs to consider the stages to implement what you need and want. These are big questions requiring detailed answers later on, but for your initial roadmap you can take a high level view to start with.

- ❑ What technology systems do you have now? Are you happy with them?
- ❑ What will you need for the future? How will you clarify and correctly specify what you need? Who will do this?
- ❑ What are the gaps? Can your current systems grow how you need them to grow?
- ❑ What can you afford?
- ❑ How can you easily get what you need?
- ❑ Is the technology available? If so, from where?
- ❑ Will you use your existing systems and keep them in-house? Will you buy new software? Will you rent software from the Cloud? Will you build your own?
- ❑ What hardware will you need?
- ❑ What budget will you need?
- ❑ What are the likely timeframes needed to find and implement the systems you need?
- ❑ What stages will make the most sense for your business?
- ❑ Do you have the right technical help to do this? Are your current internal IT team and external partners right for the job?

There is a detailed section further in this book on Choosing Technology, so check there for more tips to follow and traps to avoid.

As a starting point, focus on software systems and solutions that are:

- ❑ Already built and available rather than those you can get custom-built just for your own business. Try to find the 100% Perfect Fit Product that is right or nearly right for your business.
- ❑ Open and not going to lock you in to a single vendor, IT company or web partner.
- ❑ Secure, Reliable, Scalable and Proven.
- ❑ Able to integrate with your other systems; now and even more so in the future.
- ❑ Easy to implement and learn.
- ❑ Low or affordable cost.
- ❑ Likely to have acceptable or potentially high Return on Investment (ROI).
- ❑ Low Risk.
- ❑ Able to provide you with high flexibility and agility.
- ❑ Likely to give you good expansion, extension and integration options for the future.

How can you create more Customer Convenience, Trust, Value and Payoff?

Step 10: Decide Your RoadMap

- Review Opportunities & Strategies
- Assess business cases for options
- Assess capabilities & resources
- Develop Big Picture view (3+ Years)
- Decide best strategies (1 & 3+ Years)
- Plan RoadMap Stages & Goals (3M, 12M, 3Y)
- Plan in 3 Month chunks

By now, you probably have many different ideas and options for your future Digital Roadmap.

Some may be new and seem outrageously radical and revolutionary.

Others could be small, incremental and evolutionary improvements or enhancements of what you are currently doing in your business.

An idea could be as simple as a minor change to your website; or it could involve a total re-development of your website. Or it could be launching a new product or digitally transforming an existing product or process.

Some ideas may make great sense to you and your customers for the future, but may appear impossible to do cost-effectively now with today's technology.

At this stage, don't discard any new ideas. Make sure you hold onto the good ideas, even those that are impossible or difficult to implement.

New technology tools evolve and appear almost daily. The technology you think is impossible could exist already somewhere in the world.

If you want to implement a really smart strategy, then finding or not finding the tools to help you do it easily could change the course of your entire business future.

Sometimes the wildest ideas are later seen to be the best ones.

After all, a crazy but totally customer-focused business idea based on powerful Digital Age Action Principles and Trends could become a successful business concept.

You don't really want a crazy new Revolutionary Competitor to implement the concept tomorrow or in 18 months time as it might be the crazy idea that puts you out of business.

Obviously there is a lot more to do to plan, implement and achieve the roadmap, but you're developing the Big Picture view that makes sense for you so you know where you are headed.

It's an on-going process. Treat your roadmap as a continually evolving work-in-progress.

Remember to maintain your customer focus. Ultimately, it's all about delivering better value to your customers with more convenience, less inconvenience, less risk, using fewer resources, and doing it faster and at a lower cost.

Work out what is important to your customers – and then give them more of what they want and less of what they don't want. Make sure it all happens with low risk, high flexibility, good options for the future and high long-term ROI.

Weighing Up Your Options

As you work through the process, you'll probably come up with lots of different ideas and options.

Group your ideas and possible strategies into categories that make sense for you. Develop a rating system to assess each of these on a scale that works for you. This can help you develop your preferred options.

It's always helpful to keep notes of your thinking processes as things change in time. At a later date, you may want to re-visit some of the options that don't make it onto your roadmap for the next 3 years.

Here are some criteria that could be helpful to you and your business to assess different options.

- Customer Value: How much will this idea be valued by the customers?
- Customer Want: How much will this idea be wanted by the customers?
- Trend Power: To what extent does this idea fit in with the Trends? How much Trend power will it have?
- Company Value: What value will this idea have for our company?
- Company Want: How much will our company want to do this idea?

- Availability of Technology: Is the technology to do this readily available today?
- Choice of Technology: What technology platforms would be needed for this idea?
- Implementation Ease: How easy would it be to implement this idea?
- Implementation Capabilities: Do we have the capabilities to implement this idea?
- Implementation Time: How long will it take to implement this idea?
- Implementation Cost: What will be the cost to implement this idea?
- Ongoing Ease: After we have this new idea implemented, how easy will it be to keep it successfully operating on an ongoing basis?
- Ongoing Capabilities: Do we have the capabilities to keep it successfully operating on an ongoing basis?
- Ongoing Cost: What will be the cost to keep it successfully operating on an ongoing basis?
- Likely Risk: What are the likely risks with this idea?
- Likely ROI – Size of Pay-off: What is the likely financial return our company would get from this idea?
- Likely ROI – Time for Pay-off: How long is it likely to be until our company gets this financial return from this idea?
- Likely ROI – Length of Payoff: How long is this financial return likely to continue from this idea?
- Likely Date For Action to Prepare: How long will it take us to prepare for this idea? What date could we start to prepare for it?
- Likely Date For Action to Launch: When would we be likely to launch this idea? What date should we launch it?

Using Your RoadMap

Your Digital RoadMap helps you see your planned journey for the next 3 years, with the next 12 months chunked into 3 month blocks to show you the important stages and goals along the way.

Use your RoadMap to help guide you and your team with the various decisions you need to make in your business.

Your RoadMap will probably be very different to that of other businesses, even businesses similar to yours.

You may have similar strategies to other businesses in your industry, but how you take action and implement your strategies will be unique for you.

You need to be alert to the actions of competitors and also to the changing environment for your customers. You may need to quickly adjust your tactics and your actions as circumstances change.

Don't be too quick to change your Big Picture view and strategies for the future, as you don't want to be reactionary in your planning. After all, that's why you have your RoadMap.

> *"The pessimist complains about the wind; the optimist expects it to change; the realist adjusts the sails."*
>
> William Arthur Ward

Overlaps: Tasks Taking Longer Than 3 Months

Some tasks will be part of projects that will overlap and stretch across more than one 3 month block.

Overlap is inevitable, but where possible try to define specific milestone goals for these overlapping tasks that can be achieved at the end of each 3 month block.

It will make managing easier and is likely to keep you and others on track so you don't have what project managers call 'slippage'. You don't want slippage. You do want "On time, on budget". Clear milestone goals help.

RoadMapping Is An Ongoing Process

Planning your Digital RoadMap for your journey for the next 3 years is NOT something to do now and then leave for the next 3 years. The RoadMap needs to be regularly updated.

The best approach is to update your RoadMap every 3 months. Review it, revise it and then roll your plans forward by a further 3 months.

Here's how it can work... Every 3 months, you:

1. Review your 3 Year Big Picture view and amend it as you want.
2. Review your 3 Year Digital Strategies and amend them, fine-tune them, improve them.
3. Review your 3 Year & 12 Month Stages and Goals. You're now 3 months into your RoadMap, so it's time to roll the stages forward by 3 months so you always have 3 Year and 12 Month Stages and Goals ahead of you.

4. Set your new 3 Year and 12 Month Stages & Goals based on your actual achievements for the past 3 months and any amendments you've made to your Big Picture and Strategies.
5. Re-define your up-coming 3 Month blocks. Ideally, you'll just be rolling forward into the next 3 months and creating the next in the series of 3 month blocks.

Your 3 Month Action Plan blocks may extend 6 or 12 months into the future, or further depending on what you want to achieve.

It's important for your plans to be ambitious, but it's usually more important for them to be realistic. We don't live in an ideal world; we live in the real world. Keep your Digital RoadMap real for your business.

You will never be able to plan every stage with total accuracy. The future doesn't work that way.

Make sure your Big Picture future view continues to makes sense. Make sure your business strategies are sound, and make sure you are progressing along your pathway.

The specific details on your roadmap will vary as you go along. You'll learn plenty of new things along the journey. There'll be new questions and they'll need new answers. You can't predict and plan for every detail.

Circumstances will change.

Part of the challenge is knowing what questions to ask yourself and others. Ask new questions, different questions, and better questions.

That's how it is in the Digital Age…

Choosing Technology

Any sufficiently advanced technology is indistinguishable from magic.

Arthur C. Clarke

We are stuck with technology when what we really want is just stuff that works.

Douglas Adams, The Salmon of Doubt

There are two primary choices in life: to accept conditions as they exist, or accept the responsibility for changing them.

Denis Waitley

Why Smart People sometimes make Dumb Choices

Faced with choosing information technology (IT), many otherwise super-smart people can make some very un-smart decisions.

Why do businesses make poor technology choices? Why do so many businesses have horror stories about IT projects that go 'off-track'? More importantly, what can we learn from them?

I don't think anyone sets out to make poor technology choices, so why does it happen?

Please note, when I talk about this with business CEOs and management teams, they usually nod in agreement with me. Most realize they need to act smarter and take responsibility for changing the way their business must operate to successfully roll-out their future digital roadmap.

I find many IT people, website developers and other digital service providers agree with my comments, but others don't. Some get a bit upset with me. I'm not trying to be a smartass, nor am I perfect myself; I've got my own horror stories and some were very painful.

My comments on IT firms also refer to software vendors and developers, web development companies and other digital service providers. Some are great; others less so. Hopefully this chapter can help you recognize the difference and learn some traps to avoid as you implement your Digital RoadMap.

Technology systems are often introduced to improve tasks or fix problem areas in a business. Being task-related or function-related can result in different technology tools being used for different tasks.

Problems arise when the tools and systems used for different tasks and functions are not able to be connected to each other.

Rather than enjoying business benefits from the integration of information, systems and processes, businesses suffer from disintegration.

Many people don't recognise disintegration for what it is; they just see that the new technology system has not improved the business much - and they blame the IT guys and IT generally.

Often there are unrealistic expectations of the benefits new systems may bring. Requirements may be undefined or loosely defined. Alternatively, plans may be overly-defined or systems chosen that are too prescriptive and regimented and become too complex or inflexible.

Other plans are far too vendor-specific, dictating the use of technology languages, platforms or products that may have been appropriate choices in the past but are now dying.

Most IT firms will benefit from locking you in to a long-term relationship with them, but being locked in to an ailing service provider or a dying software product is frightening as you need support, flexibility and agility for the future.

Many businesses have questionable or non-existent internal IT project management skills or unrealistic expectations of project management from already busy people employed to do something else in their'real job'.

Doubtful forecasting doesn't help. Add in the inability of those involved to achieve naïvely forecast 'Best-Case' or 'Likely-Case' scenarios and expectations of budgets and delivery timeframes, and you have a recipe for projects going off-track, and often quickly - but it gets worse.

The 'Project' View

Perhaps somewhat paradoxically, many IT projects go off-the-rails because they are treated as'projects'.

Taking a'project' view often encourages a silo mentality. Internal boundaries are put around a project to define it; sometimes to make it manageable but often so the project can be quickly progressed without needing to involve too many other people, especially others who may have conflicting interests.

Be careful how you define different IT projects your business may be rolling out. For most businesses, very few IT systems stand alone without connections to other processes and systems. Integration beats fragmentation, so consider the interaction points between different processes as you plan projects.

Different Departments Speak Different Languages

Managing projects with conflicting interests is challenging, especially when communication and trust levels are not high within an organization.

I've seen this happen both within departments and between departments within a firm, where the people involved either don't talk to each other much or don't like each other much. And yes, it still happens.

A common departmental battle is between Marketing & IT. Not only do they often not talk to each other; when they do talk, they usually speak in different languages.

When marketing and IT do battle, the result for customers can be a dysfunctional mess. Customer-facing IT processes become cumbersome and inefficient. IT system breakdowns annoy customers and cost money. As the business owner, inter-departmental battles are the last thing you want.

Scope Creep

Probably the biggest issue is "Scope-Creep" where project deliverables shift during the project. This is typically caused by a combination of poorly defined initial requirements and a lack of understanding from the business about what they are buying and getting with the new system.

Scope Requirements Change As Knowledge Grows

The business owner (or management team) usually learns a lot during the course of the project, and as they learn more, they develop a clearer understanding of what they want. The requirements may need to be changed, but changing is not always easy.

Problems arise when the customer disagrees with the IT firm about the expectations of what was to be delivered in the original project.

Some IT firms intentionally prolong this customer ignorance rather than making a point of clearly defining requirements initially.

Some IT firms count on scope creep happening and actively encourage it, especially when they can vary the price. In some situations, the contractual fine-print allows the IT firm to make seemingly massive price variations for relatively minor changes.

Scope variations end up either costing more money or creating drama if the customer and the IT firm can't agree on resolving the variations. IT firms may slow down or terminate a fixed price job where scope variations continually cause customer disagreements.

Technology Soup Du Jour

Some business managers shift from one technology fad to another. It's like they are selecting a new Technology Soup Du Jour (Soup Of The Day) from a different menu every day just so they can appear up to date and using the latest techno-buzzword.

This can get very confusing within an organization. It pays to recognize Technology Soup for what it is… and to learn not to order the soup yourself. Don't let others order it either.

Technology Soup can be very expensive, leave a bad taste in your mouth, and generally makes you and your business sick – sometimes for months or years to come.

People tire of constantly shifting to the next best thing in technology; it's unhelpful and adds to the problem of The Blur.

Planning your business based on the latest fads and gadgets makes for ad-hoc short-term planning, bad decisions, confusion and generally poor results.

It's another powerful argument for developing your Digital RoadMap and updating it every 3 months.You stay up to date in a planned way and add new tools to your business without adding to The Blur.

It usually pays to be open about the choice of technology and tools you could use. Don't just stay with what you have for the sake of it, but don't change just for the sake of it either.

Look at what you need the system to be able to do for your business and more importantly, for your customers. Understand the range of new tools and the new capabilities these tools provide, and decide how this capability can be used in your business. Add this to your RoadMap.

IT Projects Are Like House Building Projects

Getting new software or a new website is a bit like you getting a house built to your requirements by a builder. Once the house structure has been built it can get pretty expensive to add some more rooms or make the kitchen bigger.

If you want a new home built, you may be able to look at pre-built display homes of your chosen builder to make sure you know exactly what you are going to get.

It's always better to have the plans clear at the start. If you leave it until the house is built to realize you need passageways between rooms, you'll probably be up for expensive changes.

If you want a unique home built, it's always smarter to engage an architect to draw up the plans exactly how you want them, and to do this before you commence laying any bricks. It's the same with software development.

If you get a good experienced architect involved, they will help you think through what you need and will ask questions about things you hadn't yet considered. They have experience, whereas you don't know what you don't know.

Create Smart Pilot Programs

A pilot program is not just proving to you that the new system can work. A good well-run pilot is a great way of changing culture and work practices within an organization.

Ideally you want the pilot to become an example to others who then willingly adopt new systems and practices rather than being forced to adopt them. This way, your new systems can have a far better take-up rate and successful rollout.

Be smart with your pilot programs. Plan them carefully, run them well, learn from them and then let the people within the pilot group promote the benefits of the pilot to others.

Expect Bias from Product Vendors

Don't expect that product vendors will give you independent advice, even if they offer you a 'free consultation'.

The sales consultants and product specialists from IT firms may be technical experts, but they are talking to you so they can make a sale. Most are going to be biased towards what they sell. Expect this bias, and learn to recognize it.

Non-Independent 'Consulting'

For many IT companies, 'consulting' becomes an opportunity to get paid for their 'pre-sales' work – assessing requirements, scoping out projects, defining specifications and yes, even making short-lists of 'suitable products'.

IT companies that are also vendors of specific products will typically recommend their own solutions where they can. In some cases, these may be exactly right for you, but how do you really know? Some IT firms will recommend their products after they have defined your requirements. They may interpret what you need so it appears a close fit to the products they can offer. This may - or may not - be the best for you.

It's often better to find independent advisors and consultants who will not be involved in the implementation of whatever solution is selected. This may cost you a bit more initially but if you make wiser choices as a result, it will usually prove to have been a smart investment.

When you do get advice from IT companies that are also going to be involved in the implementation, check their references and reference sites very carefully as part of your selection process.

The better companies will typically ask you a series of questions up-front to find out if their product is likely to be a good fit for you.

You and Your Budget

One of the key questions will be about your budget. You may have a very tight budget with real constraints or you may have plenty of money available. You may not know how much you want to spend and you probably won't know how much – or how little – you need to spend to get what you want and need.

Unless you have unlimited funds, it's always best if you give your prospective IT firms some guidance about the range of money you will be happy to invest.

Different solutions emerge for different price points. Low cost and high Return On Investment (ROI) is possible. You don't have to settle for high cost and an unknown ROI. Some very effective solutions could be available at what previously would have been a very low cost.

Providing prospective IT firms with a budget range usually saves both you and them wasting time if it is obvious that their system options are not the right fit for you and your price range.

Your IT People May Add To Your Risks

Rather than helping you make better long-term strategic choices, your internal Information Technology staff and technical specialists could actually increase the risks of your business making poor decisions.

Don't Blindly Leave Selection To Your "IT Experts"

You may not understand the technical details but don't blindly leave the choice of systems up to your IT staff or advisors.

If and when their choice turns out to have been a poor one, you and your business will probably suffer more than these IT 'experts' will.

If you are going to suffer from poor decisions, then get involved in the decision-making process, share in the responsibility for selection and learn from the process.

Blinkered Views

Many IT people, especially those working internally within a single organization for several years or more, can unknowingly suffer from restricted vision.

They can have a blinkered view of the world. They see what is rather than what could be or should be. They know what they know, but they may not know what you need them to know.

Your IT people will have valuable experience of your business and your IT systems. This is usually helpful, but when it comes to fresh views on new solutions, this historical experience can work against you. Many people have a bias towards working with - and buying more of - what they already know and understand.

If the best solution for you is to get the next version of your current systems, then your internal staff can help. This may not require a 'big decision', but you still want to make sure it is the best decision.

Knowledge Gaps

If the best solution for the future is something you don't know about yet, your current internal staff may not be the right people to help you find it.

If the best new system requires deep knowledge of new programming languages and this is knowledge they don't have, then your current IT people may feel threatened and insecure in their roles. At best they may not be able to help in the selection of your new solutions; at worst, they may actively sabotage your selection processes. (I've seen it happen.)

Fearing For Their Jobs

If the best new system involves working with technology platforms that are Cloud-based or pre-built software that is easily able to be deployed and implemented with little or no customization work, some of your IT people may think they will no longer be required and may think they will be made redundant. They may be right.

Your good problem-solvers who thrive on challenges may feel unappreciated and unfulfilled. In time, they may become bored and leave. You will probably want them to stay.

If you do find products that are a perfect fit for your business, then make sure your key IT people know they will still have a valuable role within your business.

The functionality of these pre-built systems may be defined already, but you still need people to keep the systems talking to each other. Integration and connectivity is critical.

Baffling with BS

From my experience, many IT people aren't good at admitting when they don't know something. (Of course, this trait is not just found in the IT industry.)

> ***"Some will try to make answers up, and others will try to 'baffle you with BS'."***

Some will try to make answers up, and others will try to 'baffle you with bullshit'. Not surprisingly, this Technical BS obviously adds extra risks to your business and leads to poor selection decisions.

The risks get worse for those business owners who naively 'trust the experts' and believe what they are being told even if it does not make sense.

You need advisors who have broad experiences across different technologies, are up -to-date with their current knowledge and who have deep and wide insightful views on the range of future technology options for your business.

Tech Experts or Business Experts?

Don't expect technical experts to be business experts.

Some IT people are very skilled and experienced business analysts who can quickly assess a business situation and define the various tasks in complex processes.

Many technical staff will find it difficult, if not impossible to draw back far enough from the technology to advise and guide you on your fundamental business strategies. Strong technicians may prefer to stay immersed in the technical world. Learn to recognize and work with their strengths.

Playing With Toys

Some IT people like to work in a fun-filled IT playground where they continually want to try new things and play with the latest toys.

Encouraging experimentation and innovation may be good, but if you frequently support your technical team in playing with new IT tools and toys, be careful what they roll out in your business.

Businesses that play with new technology systems can learn plenty of new things but can often waste time and money without measurable results. It's better to play first and add new tools to your RoadMap in a structured and disciplined approach.

Document the IT Magic Tricks

We all know that a good magician doesn't often tell you how they do their clever tricks... but many IT people make a point of keeping their tricks to themselves.

The more tricks they know and the less you know, the more powerful is their hold over you... and that can become very dangerous for you.

IT magicians may not like sharing their tricks but you need them to document their magic

Keeping your business running in the digital age does not require magic and it should not require luck or you being over-exposed to preventable danger. You want to make sure no one holds you and your business to ransom by withholding knowledge from you.

If your IT person decides to move on from your business, then knowledge handovers should be easy to manage. They seldom are.

You need documented systems that anyone can follow. You need passwords, processes and practices written down and securely stored.

Make sure adequate documentation of the Magic systems is done well in advance of you needing the documentation. Get someone independent to check the documentation for completeness and accuracy. It's important; this could make or break your entire business.

Challenges With Software

All Software Has Bugs

You may not realize it, but all software has bugs; some are more critical than others, and you will encounter some bugs far more often than others.

Look at the lists of known bugs in the software you are considering, and look to see how quickly these bugs are fixed by the software developers or the user communities.

Check The Development Path For The Software

Look for the future roadmap for that software. Don't just look at what may be planned or promised for the future, but look at the track record of the developers in achieving their past plans and promises.

What Support Will You Get?

Make sure you choose software developers and implementation partners who have a strong reputation for providing great support. Sooner or later you will need it, and in some cases, great IT support could also make or break your business success.

Check with other users of the software who have needs and requirements similar to yours. Find out the strengths and weaknesses of the software. Check the online user groups for support for that software.

Look For Near 100% Perfect Fit Solutions

Too many people choose their technology before they really know what they need the technology to do for them. They settle for what a system can do, and then compromise their business processes to suit the technical system they have.

Plan your business – and then get the technology to suit you. You may still need to get some software custom-built, but it's always smarter to find software that is already a great fit with what you need – and then get small and relatively minor customizations done to the software to make it better fit your business.

In the future it's more likely you will be able to find exactly what you need. Define your requirements and how you want the system to work. Research software for your industry and learn what is available and what functionality is becoming available for your type of business.

In a world of 100% Perfect Fit niche solutions, the perfect system could be out there somewhere. You can try to find it – or let it find you by asking questions in your community.

How Can Your Business Be Unique?

There are many pre-built software systems you can buy or use, especially for your business websites and mobile apps. If you use the same website-building system that your competitors use, then how will your business be unique?

You can present your business as unique with clever innovative design and your unique content, but you can also differentiate by using additional functionality you've had specially built for your customers to use. How you add different components with synergy can create your uniqueness.

> ***Plan your business and then get the technology to suit you***

With a good proven system providing the core operational platform for your website, you could use extra functionality you get specially built or integrated into the core system to make sure your customers can do smarter things on your website than they can on your competitors' websites.

If everyone in your industry uses the same techno-tools, then clearly the technology itself will not be a differentiator between businesses. There is often comfort in using the industry standard software for your type of business, as long as it does what you need and helps you achieve your own unique business roadmap.

There is a vast difference between having a tool and knowing how to use it well. Even bigger differences become obvious when you add varying levels of customer service to the mix.

Your business may never be unique based on your technology, but how well you use your IT systems may help define your uniqueness.

If you are inefficient, technology will highlight that inefficiency on a bigger scale.

Jonar Nadar

Implement in Phases

You can't do everything at once, so don't try to. Plan on implementing your new systems in phases. Start with a pilot if you need to, and learn from the pilot before proceeding.

Many businesses don't know what they want to learn from a pilot project, so they end up not learning much at all. Decide in advance what you want to find out during and after the pilot. Plan how you will measure success and failure, and define your goals and objectives.

Use the successes of the pilot to promote the benefits of the new system to your prospective users, whether they are your customers, your staff or your ecosystem.

Selecting the right systems can be a massive part of the challenge of implementing your Digital RoadMap. You want the system to be right for today and tomorrow and to give you the flexibility to grow for your future.

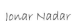

21 Tips for Making Smarter Technology Choices

If you are planning a new website or selecting some new technology system, you can make smarter selection decisions if you know what to look for and what to avoid.

Choosing the wrong system gets expensive for your business even if it is free.

Consider these 21 points early in your selection process to help you stay agile and flexible on your pathway.

This will help you save time, money and stress now as well as giving you the best options for the future.

Look for a new system that is:

1. Functional and able to do what you need it to do.

Clearly defining your own requirements is probably the hardest step in the selection process. You can spend a lot of time analyzing your own business processes, issues and the outcomes you need from the system.

It's a never-ending process which will evolve as your business, your customers and your technology options evolve.

Prioritizing your requirements into features that are either "Essential Now, Nice to Have Now, Essential Later, and Nice to Have Later" can be a good start.

Unless your needs are simple or your budget unlimited, you will find your selection will always involve some compromises and clearly knowing the important business outcomes you want to achieve is the key.

2. Easy to learn.

If a new system looks cluttered, cumbersome and hard to use, it probably is.

Good software looks easy to use. It's not accidental – good software is designed and built with novice users in mind rather than just catering to highly trained and experienced users.

You may need some basic training, but most good well-designed software will appear to be intuitive and relatively easy to start to use.

3. Able to be trialed.

Don't just commit to using a new system. Trial it, run a pilot program and learn from it.

Have clear boundaries for the trial and know how and when you will judge the trial to be a success.

If you jump in too deeply and start using a system too broadly in your pilot phase with lots of real customers, it can be hard to extract yourself from the system later.

Be careful, as vendors have a vested interest in making the trial successful. They may be hoping that you lock yourself into the system during the free trial period.

4. Efficient & Effective.

The new system must help you do what you need to do quickly and easily, and preferably better than how you are doing things at the moment.

The software should be efficient, and it should make you and your team more efficient, more effective and more productive.

Think how you can measure the increases in efficiency, effectiveness and productivity.

Develop these measures and use them as performance indicators and to determine the Return On Investment (ROI) you are making.

Most businesses don't do this – and they are left wondering if the new system really did make such a difference.

5. Extensible and Scalable.

Your new system must be capable of being extended and preferably have a large number of readily available plug-in applications available for your use.

Scalability is vital as the system will need to be able to easily grow with you or easily shrink with you if your needs diminish.

6. Open, Integratable and Secure.

You may not know it now, but sooner or later you will want to connect other things (databases, software apps, processes, etc) to your system.

Will it be easy, hard or impossible? Who will be needed to do this integration work and how secure will the connections be?

7. Accessible for mobile users.

Almost any type of system you consider these days will need to have some parts of it available for mobile users who might be accessing the system and its capabilities through a smartphone, tablet or other wireless device.

Encourage mobility for your customers and your staff.

8. Already in use by a large base of users.

A large and happy user base will give you confidence in your selection and people to turn to for extra help.

It's also more likely that the product will continue to survive and evolve if lots of others love it and depend on it.

Depending on the importance of the system to you, you may want to talk to other users and ask them about their experiences with the product and the vendor.

Join the User Groups for these products and start asking questions about the product, the support services and the known bugs with the product – and how responsive the vendor is to fixing these bugs.

9. Popular in credible reviews.

Use peer reviews and recommendations. Don't blindly follow others, but don't ignore them either.

10. Showing positive momentum in the marketplace with a credible future development roadmap.

Products, like people are either green and growing or ripe and rotting. You want to choose a growing product.

It's usually best to find a software product with a planned development roadmap that is public knowledge, and not just in the minds of developers somewhere.

Check out the track record of the vendors and developers and see how they have fulfilled their previously announced roadmaps.

Software development is not easy, and keeping up with ongoing product development is a challenge for many software firms, especially small ones. Don't just assume that what may be good today will continue to be maintained and kept good for tomorrow.

11. Backed by a strong development community.

The more people who are actively involved collaboratively in the development of the product, the better it is likely to be – but only if it has a well-managed roadmap to protect the core system from too many changes that creating confusing branches of product development.

Choose a product with a carefully managed core product and avoid products with too many branches in their development roadmap.

12. Common Language based.

You want software written in a common programming language so you have a large base of technical skills available.

13. Well Supported BEFORE you buy it.

You can't just rely on information you find on some vendor's website.

You want someone to be able to answer your questions. It's important to be able to ask intelligent questions and get intelligent answers during your investigative research and shopping process.

It's also important for you to be able to ask questions that might be dumb – and get an intelligent, helpful and guiding response.

You don't want to be made to feel like a fool by some sales dude who is too busy or too remote to care.

Use the pre-sales support you receive as a guide to how your relationship with this vendor might be after the sale.

(In my experience, a business that does not care about you during the sales process won't magically start to care about you AFTER you've paid your money to them.)

14. Well supported AFTER you buy it.

Depending on the size and capabilities of your team, you may want or need good local support or you may be happy enough to have remote support provided online by others.

Don't assume that the people on your own IT team will always be there; in fact, make contingency plans for if and when they leave.

Some products may not need much support at all, but make sure you choose systems where external technical support is readily available.

Find out who will provide it, at what cost and in what response time. Find out what a support contract will include and exclude.

Software support is a bit like insurance. It's better to have it and not need it, than need it and not have it. Just like insurance, you only really know how good it is when you have to make a claim.

Check it – and talk to other customers about their experiences.

15. Able to be quickly installed.

Ideally installation of software should be easy and preferably through an automated process.

If software has or needs complex installation procedures, then be wary of it as it is likely to also need complex training and support, and that can get expensive later on.

In the Cloud computing environment, with hosted Software as a Service (SaaS) solutions, there are no installation issues and no infrastructure you need to buy, but there are other issues about data ownership and access, privacy and long-term costs to consider. (Some of these have been raised in the Trend discussions on Low Cost Software & Cloud Computing.)

16. Not always going to require Expensive Experts to help you.

Popular software systems are often popular because they are already functional and easy to use.

If you are looking at SaaS software or Cloud solutions, it may not be possible to get modifications made so the software exactly meets your needs, but ideally software you choose should be relatively easy to have modified.

This will require technical expertise, but preferably not expertise that is only available from a very small number of seriously clever and expensive experts.

It can be very reassuring when you know you're not locked in to future relationships if they go sour. You won't enjoy being continually at the mercy of a software vendor who has a monopoly hold over you. Even needing other hard-to-find external technical expertise can become problematic.

17. Good value initially.

Low cost generally beats high cost, but it's all relative. The question is more about value.

Sometimes the initial cost might be free and plenty of great open source software is available online for free.

Look for the catch, as relying on free commercial products can often be in the 'too good to be true' category.

Some free software may actually contain viruses or other mal-ware. Don't blindly download free software.

Don't be put off by good products being free, and don't assume free or cheap is good or bad. Look at reviews from others you trust and test the software yourself.

18. Good value for its Lifetime.

Consider the likely Total Cost of Ownership (TCO) of a system you are looking to introduce.

TCO includes costs associated with

a. computer hardware and programs for your network, servers, devices, warranties and licenses, migration expenses, upgrades, patches and future licensing policies, etc.

b. operating expenses such as electricity, testing costs, downtime, outage and failure expenses, security (including breaches, loss of reputation, recovery and prevention), backup and recovery processes, technology training, implementation, insurance and even future upgrade expenses and decommissioning.

19. Migratable.

Your new systems need to be relatively easy for you to migrate into, and VERY easy for you to get out of later if and when you want to cease using the system.

Never use an external hosted service that does not promise to give you your data back when you want to leave.

20. Gives your business good options for the future.

Despite some techos using the term future-proof, no technology system really is.

Look for standards, languages and platforms that are popular with enough of a critical mass of users to have continual development and enhancement even if the company that currently owns the system goes broke.

Your business will need flexibility and agility to survive and grow

Make sure the technology you implement today can be easily adapted for changing processes in your business in months and years to come.

Your business will need flexibility and agility to survive and grow. Your technology must help you and not hinder you as your business evolves.

21. Low Risk.

All systems carry some level of risk but you don't need to willingly take high risks in your choice of technology,

Don't fall for the slick promises of tech sales guys, and don't believe everything you are told.

You can't avoid risk – so make a list of the possible risks for each of the various options you are considering and plan how you will mitigate and reduce these risks.

Making Decisions

It's often said that in business, it is better to make a bad decision than to make no decision.

When it comes to selecting new technology, it can get tough. No one intentionally tries to make bad selection decisions, but with the benefit of hindsight, many people find their past decisions weren't really smart, and sometimes they were downright wrong.

Making technology selection decisions that turn out to be wrong can be much worse than staying with the status quo of continuing to use your existing systems.

Poor technology choices can add stress and waste plenty of money and time. Worse, you waste opportunities, especially if customers move away from you as a result of ineffective, error-ridden or insecure systems.Your business goodwill can reduce or evaporate.

If you can't find a new alternative that is better than what you currently have, then it may be better to stay with what you currently have. It's worth realizing that deciding NOT to make a selection decision is in fact a decision in itself.

It is okay to decide to continue to use business systems that are still functioning for your business, even if new technology options present themselves.

> ***Don't let technology sales guys or evangelists take you down a wrong pathway***

Don't let the technology sales guys or even well-meaning technology evangelists both inside and outside your business lead you or push you down a pathway that does not help your business and your customers.

Having said all of that, when you do make decisions to select new technology, you learn new things. You get in motion rather than stagnation.

The motion needs to be along your chosen pathway; your business needs to be progressing on your Digital Roadmap.

When you are in motion, especially in motion along your RoadMap, then you will find yourself continually trying new things. The key is to try these new things and learn from them – and then make continual improvement corrections along the pathway.

> ***Stay ahead of your customers' expectations***

You need to stay ahead of your customers' expectations. If making a decision to stay with old technology and old business practices puts you behind the wants and expectations of your customers, then this decision in itself will add plenty of risk to your business.

From my experience, deciding to focus on your customers first will always help you make the best decisions you can at the time. Mistakes that genuinely help your customers will seldom be serious mistakes. Learn from everything you do. Fail Fast, and Fail Forward.

Your Journey

This is the true joy in life, the being used for a purpose recognized by yourself as a mighty one; the being thoroughly worn out before you are thrown on the scrap heap; the being a force of Nature instead of a feverish selfish little clod of ailments and grievances complaining that the world will not devote itself to making you happy.

George Bernard Shaw

Live your life each day as you would climb a mountain. An occasional glance towards the summit keeps the goal in mind, but many beautiful scenes are to be observed from each new vantage point.

Harold B. Melchart

Failure is never easy and success is never permanent. The key is the courage to continue forward.

Winston Churchill

You Can Do It

There's a lot to cover as you plan your business future in the Digital Age. Please don't be daunted and put off by the work involved. (It can be fun really…)

Remember,

- Choose your path. You can't do everything;
- Choose your helpers. You can't do it yourself; and
- Choose your stages. You can't do it all at once.

Develop your business in stages. The journey of a thousand miles begins with the first step, and the best way to eat an elephant is one bite at a time.

Some strategies will instantly make real sense for your business. Others will not be for you. Open your mind and your open your eyes, but also trust your gut feelings.

See the Big Picture future for your industry and your business first so you know where you are heading before you take action.

Remember, planning in a changing landscape is an ongoing process. Act smarter with your digital business strategies.

Just having a website is not enough. If your website is really to be an important part of your business, then you keep it up to date and growing – just like your business.

Plan for change. Base your business strategies on things that won't change, and on change you can predict.

Everything changes in time especially in the digital world, so your business planning depends on your planning time-frame and horizons.

Make sure your website and your online activities support your strategies. Systems, platforms, tactics and tools change frequently. Wisely choose those that will support your long-term plans. Do more of what works. Build your experience and your capabilities.

Invest in convenience. Improve your systems to increase customer convenience.

Be ahead of your customers. Understand the expectations of your key customers and make sure you are ahead of them

At the minimum in the digital online world, you have to meet the online needs, wants and expectations of your current key customers. If you do, life goes on. If you don't, then sooner or later your customers will leave you. (Sorry, but that's how it is.)

Many businesses will struggle with customers using different channels to reach them and interact with them online. These different sales channels such as your website, mobile, phone, catalogue and in-store all need to be able to work for you.

Think of each of these sales channels as part of the pathways for your customers to do business with you.

Create different pathways leading to your business. Encourage customers to use whatever pathway is best for them at the time. Let your customers use whatever is most convenient for them.

Use Video where possible. Text and photos are important, but video can be very convenient for some customers. Video can build trust and credibility faster, so provide short, relevant, helpful videos.

You don't have to spend a lot of money on videos. Learn the basics and you can probably make your videos yourself.

Video showing you and your team as sincere, authentic caring people who know what you are doing and are trustworthy will be better for you than some slick professional piece that may look good to you but may not appear 'real' to your customers.

Encourage Customer Reviews. Follow up your customers after the sale to make sure they're happy. Ask them to write about their experiences with you and add these to your website.

Build Trust. Add Trust Builders to your website and remove anything that could reduce trust in you. Eliminate these Trust Busters.

Make Word-of-Mouth your friend. Some people will always talk. Others prefer to listen. Find the Social Networking "Influencers" and support them. Encourage their influence. Start conversations. Engage with others. Add value to conversations. Respond kindly.

Grow your Community. Find out where your customers go online. Join, belong and add value to your niche communities online.

Become one of the trusted suppliers to your community. Your community becomes your marketplace.

Use Magnetic Leverage. Become a magnet for the sort of customers you want. Build your networks to attract customers to your site and stores.

Be Mobile-friendly. Cater to customers with mobile devices. Let them quickly find what they want from you when they're mobile. Have a mobile website that is smart for smartphone users. Try to keep your mobile site integrated with your main website to re-use content and use the same content management system. Maintenance is easier.

> **A bend in the road is not the end of the road... unless you fail to turn.**
>
> Anon

Reward referrals well. Build strong referral systems and build your own affiliate sales network. Be happy to pay commissions on sales from your affiliates.

Be Contactable. Make sure customers can find you and call you. Sometimes people look up websites just to find your phone number or business address. Unless you're trying to hide, make your contact details easy to find. (If you are selling online and trying to hide from your customers, quit now and go do something else.)

Use Guarantees. Have good guarantees and honor them. Win on Delivery. Make delivery fast, simple and trackable.

Get smarter with technology. Use tech systems that are proven, open, integratable, well-supported and ideally non-proprietary.

Free does not mean bad. Free also does not mean good. Expensive does not mean good.

If something is free online, then ask yourself if you are paying for something in a currency other than money. Facebook is free, but you pay by giving them your private personal information.

Improve your CRM. Build and use your customer database. Build your mailing lists and customer profiles. Segment your lists and target each segment with relevant offers.

Measure to Improve. Remove the guesswork with smarter metrics. Keep your dashboard simple. Check it frequently.

Simplify Everything. Make it easy. Make it fast. Make it simple to buy and use.

Become remarkable. Give your happy customers something to talk about, and encourage them to talk.

Provide extraordinary Customer Service. This alone will help make you remarkable and will go a long way to guaranteeing your success.

Keep your promises. In a world where many others don't seem to care, just keeping your agreements and promises can make you remarkable.

Even with the best made plans, things can stuff up and you fall into unproductive guilt. If you are unable to meet a proposed deadline or promise, then let the other party know BEFORE the first agreement time expires and set a new agreement. Provided you set a new agreement before the original expires, you may be able to maintain trust even though you did not meet the original expectations.

Stay positive. Don't listen to negativity around you or in the news. Don't let negativity in others stop you from trying new things.

Negativity has been around for years. Rise above it and encourage your people to be positive for the future.

We all have doubts and fears. We live in an uncertain world. That's how it is. Here's a quote from William Shakespeare...

"Our doubts are traitors,
And make us lose the good we oft might win
By fearing to attempt."

William Shakespeare
"Measure for Measure"

Please don't be frightened to attempt. You can create the future you want for your business. You won't do it alone, and you don't need to do it alone. It's ok to ask for help.

Ask for help online and you often get it in abundance, so let the abundance of the digital world work for you.

"How's Business?"

What do you say when someone asks you, "How's business?" How do you respond? What does the little voice inside your head say to you?

How about your employees? How would they respond if someone asked them, "How's business?" What would their little voices be saying to each of them?

Do you think these voices are helping your team create the future you want?

How about your customers? What do your customers hear about your business from you and your employees?

As you embark on the planning and journey of your Digital RoadMap, you'll probably find you want to change the thinking, attitudes and actions of some of the people in your team.

From time to time, you'll probably also want to remind yourself that new things are possible and that change is worth persevering with as you move along your pathway and meet the obstacles you'll invariably encounter.

Let me share a story with you... It's from my past, but it may be helpful for you now.

Back in 1990, I owned a small publishing company. Our main product was a business magazine with ideas, inspiration and information for business owners and managers.

The magazine was sold nationally in news agencies but primarily on subscription. Our primary revenue source was advertising sales in the magazine, and sales had become a lot tougher as Australia was in an economic recession.

The recession was real. Negativity was becoming pervasive in the marketplace. Many businesses were talking negatively about the present and the future, and some in our advertising sales team were starting to believe this negativity.

As the Editor of the magazine, I could choose to believe it too. Every day I would find myself talking with business owners who were struggling and frankly, our business was barely profitable at the time.

Every day, I would also find myself talking with some business owners who were positive and excited about the future. Their businesses were doing well, and they could see opportunities where many others just saw'doom and gloom'.

It wasn't that some industry sectors were succeeding while others were failing. In every sector, some businesses were positive and doing well and others negative and struggling.

Part of the difference was attitude, but it was more than that. It was creativity, innovation and customer focus. It was also belief; belief that resulted in actions.

Those who believed they could have a brighter future were choosing to create the future they wanted. It was their choice. Those with negative beliefs had different action.

The positive people believed they could do something, and the negative people believed they couldn't do something. Both were generally right!

Everyone has a choice of what they believe, how they think, how they view the world, and how they act. Everyone has a choice how they talk and what they say when they respond to others.

All this may seem obvious to you, but back then it took me a while to realize it. When I did, I also realized we had to get creative, innovative and far more customer-focused in our own business. We also had to start changing our thoughts and beliefs; and our language and actions.

We talked about this as a team. I clearly didn't have all the answers, but we had a good team and we felt our magazine was doing something worthwhile in the marketplace. Together we came up with some new concepts, plans and programs that customers wanted to buy, and we kept the business going and growing.

It wasn't easy, especially in the face of negativity. We needed to fight the negativity, but you can't just fight negativity. You have to replace it with constructive and credible positivity that results in positive actions.

I wrote a note for our team to help support and reinforce the positive beliefs, language and actions I could see we needed to encourage. It was an affirmation for our team and the individuals in it.

We needed to change our thinking, and especially we needed to change the language our team was using to talk about our business and the state of business generally.

When someone asked any of our team, "How's business?" I wanted each of them to respond by saying "Business is great!" I also wanted the people on our team to sincerely believe that our business actually was great.

So, that's what I called the note.

It worked well for us. We had a common and shared attitude to reinforce to each other, and we had some new language to reinforce it as well.

> ***What do you say when someone asks you, "How's business?"***

The people on our team suggested we share the note with our magazine readers and customers. We printed it on a sheet of paper and sent it out with the magazine.

The feedback was positive. Many businesses kept the note, and for weeks and months afterwards we heard various stories how different businesses had mounted it in picture frames to display on their walls.

It even attracted new customers to our business, although that was never its purpose.

I wrote that note over 20 years ago, but I kept it. I sent it to someone just the other day who appreciated it. He said it helped him. You can read it now.

Business Is Great

In this office business is great.

For us the 'economy' is speeding up, not slowing down. Our business is booming!

Outside, some of the herd are talking themselves into a 'recession'. Many actually seem to enjoy it.

They are slowing down and complaining. They are wallowing in the mud of financial self-pity. For them the 'economy' provides a convenient and comfortable excuse for failure.

But we are not part of the herd!

Every day we discover new ways to provide better service and even greater value for our customers. And every day new customers are attracted to us.

They thrive on our positive attitudes, our ideas and our customer-focus. They want to share our enthusiasm!

Of course it's not always easy, but we are creative, clever and hard-working. We know our goals and we enjoy the vision of what our future success will bring.

We actively look for new opportunities, and every day we find exciting and profitable ways to help us achieve our goals.

We are not part of the herd.
For us, business is great!

So here we are today. Some parts of the world are in deep recessions. Others parts are doing better.

In every part of the world, just like back in 1990 in Australia, some businesses are doing well while others are struggling.

Business is happening online, and in the process every industry is being transformed.

In every industry, some smart businesses are creating the future they want. Others are suffering and even dying, often slowly and with unnecessary stress and pain.

With the right plans and the right help, your business can do better online. Your business can be great. You don't have to be part of the herd.

You choose your words and you choose your thoughts. You can choose your goals, strategies and your results. It's up to you.

How's business? It's your choice.

"Business Is Great" can be downloaded for free in PDF or Word format from www.SmarterWebStrategies.com.

If you like it, please use it. Pass it on to your friends, colleagues and employees. Print it out. Stick it up on your wall. Share it. Use it to inspire yourself, your team and your customers. Get it visible. Believe it. Live it.

Use it to make sure you stay away from the herd.

Where To From Here?

If *Catching Digital* has been helpful for you and you'd like to learn more, please visit my website. You'll find additional resources for planning and implementing your Digital RoadMap using smarter web strategies.

Perhaps you'd like some independent and unbiased assistance to help you in your journey. The website has details on the guidance and coaching programs I provide for business owners, CEOs and company boards locally and around the world.

From time to time, I run workshops and seminars and give conference presentations in Australia and internationally. If you would like to come along or wish to plan an event for your team, please get in touch.

Thanks for reading this book. I hope your Digital RoadMap helps you create the future you want with a journey you enjoy.

Hollywood mogul Samuel Goldwyn once said, *"The harder I work the luckier I get."* Personally, I prefer this quote attributed to Henry Ford: *"The harder and smarter I work, the luckier I get."*

Either way, I wish you good luck. Knowledge might be power, but only when you take action.

All the best
Richard Keeves

Twitter: @RichardKeeves
www.SmarterWebStrategies.com
August 2012

Acknowledgements

I am deeply grateful and indebted to friends and colleagues for their inputs and contributions over the years, and especially to those who assisted in the creation of *Catching Digital.*

Catching Digital started out as a small ebook called the *Digital TrendCatcher Guide*. I re-wrote the ebook partly as it was getting out-of-date, but more importantly because my planning processes have evolved. The Trends are much the same. The digital business planning methodology has been greatly enhanced. Smarter Digital RoadMaps are the result.

Many thanks to George Aveling, James Bull and Brian Sher for telling me the old book could have been a lot better. *Catching Digital* is a bit like the Digital Age; it's a work in progress really and part of my journey.

Thanks also go to many others who have directly or indirectly helped along the way, including Colin Atkinson, Wayne Spencer, John Clegg, Tony Walton, Janet Schramm, Laurel Papworth, Garret Dixon, Michel Hogan, John Warrilow, Mark Douglas, Ashley Whitworth, Shane Kelly, Jim Wyatt, Graham Harvey, Anne Petch, Daniel Priestley, Natalie Lincolne, Mark Garner, Jason Van Orden, Jeff Walker, Paul Dunn, Andrew Hanna, Dr Shaun Ridley, Rob Donkersloot, Miles Burke, Richard Bone, Stephen Rice, Anthony Toop, Denny Sterley, Larry Quick, Dr Wade Halvorson, David Shelton, David Barnes, Ann Macbeth, David Dell, Ian Jones, Joel Pulido, and not least, my wife Jane Keeves. Let's continue to ride waves together.

Other major influencers on my views of the Digital Age have been Nicholas Negroponte, Daniel Burrus, John Naisbitt, Ray Hammond, Tim Ferris, Dr Stephen R Covey, Blair Singer, Martha Rogers, Geoffrey Moore, Stephen M.R. Covey, Dr Edward De Bono, Anita Roddick, and Buckminster Fuller.

Among my most significant early influencers was Robert Kiyosaki, who in about 1991-2 was guest speaker at a breakfast my business magazine was hosting in Perth. Robert's seemingly simple but deeply profound message to everyone present over 20 years ago was "Your Competition Is Electronic". I've learnt so much from Robert over the years, and it was a privilege to have him as a teacher for many seminars and workshops in the 90s.

As far as I know, whatever facts quoted throughout are correct as at the time of writing. The opinions and views are my own, but many are shared with other people. Any mistakes are just mine.

Thanks again to all those who have helped with comments, suggestions, criticisms and ideas. Please keep them coming…

Many thanks

Richard

About The Author

Richard Keeves is an independent digital strategist and business advisor. He is a digital business guide for CEOs and senior management teams as well as an accomplished speaker, trainer and author.

Richard was the founder and Managing Director of the Internet Business Corporation Ltd from its missionary beginnings in 1995 to its successful sale in 2008. IBC was one of Australia's first and longest-lasting web consulting, web development and digital marketing businesses with a diverse client base locally, nationally and internationally.

Prior to IBC, from 1987 to 1995 Richard was the founder, Managing Director and Editor of Business Directions, the Perth-based nationally distributed SME business magazine.

In 1991-92, Richard conducted early research into the future of electronic publishing and electronic business. In 1993, Richard's publishing company was selected for the Australian government's Best Practice Demonstration Program which extended his research program globally, and resulted in Richard becoming an early evangelist for the strategic use of the Internet in business in 1994-95.

Richard has been prominent in the Internet industry in Australia since its early commercialization. He was the keynote speaker at the ground-breaking Information Superhighway Conference in Sydney in 1995 and since then has spoken at Internet business seminars, conference and workshops throughout Australia, New Zealand, the USA and in Asia.

Richard was President of the Western Australian Internet Association from 2004 to 2008. He has served on various industry boards and committees including the Australian Information Industry Association and the Information Industry Forum. He was a Founding Board member of the ICT Industry Collaboration Centre and was the Chair of the Ecommerce Special Interest Group for the Australian Institute of Management.

Richard is a Fellow of the Australian Institute of Management, a Fellow of the Australian Institute of Company Directors, and a Fellow of the Customer Service Institute of Australia.

Richard's deep insights on the Digital Age, his business focus and his straight talking approach makes him in demand as an advisor, workshop presenter and keynote conference speaker.

Richard's website SmarterWebStrategies.com provides a variety of smarter business resources to help business owners and managers plan and implement their Digital RoadMaps.

He provides independent advice and guidance on digital strategy, website planning, technology selection and web partner selection. See Richard's USA on the final page.

Visit www.SmarterWebStrategies.com

Follow Richard on Twitter: @RichardKeeves

A Few More Thoughts...

"Failure is never easy and success is never permanent. The key is the courage to continue forward."

Winston Churchill

"Failure is the opportunity to begin again more intelligently."

Henry Ford

"What we fear comes to pass more speedily than what we hope."

Publilius Syrus

"No one has an exclusive on opportunity. When the sun rises, it rises for everyone."

Chinese Proverb

"Our minds can shape the way a thing will be because we act according to our expectations."

Federico Fellini

"The pessimist complains about the wind; the optimist expects it to change; the realist adjusts the sails."

William Arthur Ward

"Some men have thousands of reasons why they cannot do what they want to, when all they need is one reason why they can."

Mary Frances Berry

"We are all pilgrims on the same journey… but some pilgrims have better road maps."

Nelson De Mille

"Expect the best, plan for the worst, and prepare to be surprised."

Denis Waitley

"Don't be afraid to give your best to what seemingly are small jobs. Every time you conquer one it makes you that much stronger. If you do the little jobs well, the big ones tend to take care of themselves."

Dale Carnegie

"Keep changing. When you're through changing, you're through."

Bruce Barton

"Live your life each day as you would climb a mountain. An occasional glance towards the summit keeps the goal in mind, but many beautiful scenes are to be observed from each new vantage point."

Harold B. Melchart

"Twenty years from now you will be more disappointed by the things that you didn't do than by the ones you did do. So throw off the bowlines. Sail away from the safe harbor. Catch the trade winds in your sails. Explore. Dream. Discover."

Mark Twain

"Be prepared to ride the cycles and trends of life; success is never permanent and failure is never final."

Brian Tracy

"Vision is the ability to see what is not yet, so you can create what never was..."

Doug Firebaugh

"What we see depends mainly on what we look for."

John Lubbock

"I cannot teach anybody anything, I can only make them think."

Socrates

"You have brains in your head.
You have feet in your shoes.
You can steer yourself any direction you choose."

Dr. Seuss, Oh, The Places You'll Go!

You know how when you talk with web companies, digital agencies and service providers, you might get their advice but you're never really sure if it's good strategic guidance or just suggestions based on what they can sell you.

This can be very confusing, especially if you're not sure what you need and you don't know what questions to ask. You waste plenty of time and money buying something that's not right, and getting locked in to the wrong system can limit your future growth.

What I do is provide a totally independent advisory service for business owners. You'll get honest, unbiased advice and guidance in your planning and selection decisions. I don't do implementation work and have no vested interests. I'm only interested in your success.

I help you focus on smarter web strategies for your business so you can create a clear and concise two-page Digital RoadMap outlining your best pathways forward.

You can use special information guides I produce to learn the right questions to ask when you talk with and engage potential service providers to make sure they deliver you the best results. I help you choose wisely for the future and avoid traps and obstacles along the way.

You can take control and make better choices with less risk so you enjoy more flexibility and better options for the future. You can have less stress with less waste and enjoy better results faster as you grow and protect your business online. You can enjoy the journey…

Richard Keeves, Smarter Web Strategies.com

40285718R00191

Made in the USA
Lexington, KY
31 March 2015